Advance Praise for *Get Urban!*
by Kyle Ezell, A.I.C.P.

"*Get Urban* provides a smart, nuanced and on-the-money look at the forces that are remaking this nation's urban centers. It is must reading for those concerned with revitalizing American cities or making their home there."

—Richard Florida, author, *Rise of the Creative Class*

"As America enters the 21st century, cities like Columbus are being reborn. Thanks to the natural creativity, energy and community of people who are rediscovering America in urban living, we are dispelling the dire predictions of past decades. *Get Urban!* captures the changes in America's urban heart, as people's lives are shaping the future of cities across the nation."

—Michael B. Coleman, mayor of Columbus, Ohio

"Kyle Ezell has written a timely and helpful reminder of the power of place and the magic of cities. *Get Urban!* is a valuable 'return to the city' guide that illuminates the many facets of city life and takes its readers on a journey of rediscovery in our urban frontiers."

**—Carol Coletta, host and producer of
public radio's "Smart City"**

"Reading this book will prepare you to make one of the most dramatic and positive changes in your life. Living the lessons of this book, you will become a contributing participant in the most phenomenal turnaround America's cities have ever known."

—Richard Sensenbrenner, Columbus City councilmember

"Kyle Ezell addresses one of the most compelling topics of our time–the joys and advantages of real city living. His book provides a wonderfully practical as well as inspirational guide to city living. I particularly enjoyed the many case studies of different neighborhoods and 'urbs' in cities around the country."

**—Charles Brewer, CEO of Atlanta's Green Street Properties and
developer of the award-winning Glenwood Park neighborhood**

"*Get Urban!* offers an entertaining and effective alternative to typical texts and classroom materials because it provides a completely different way to look at cities. Even those who teach urban classes may find themselves looking at cities in a new light! Add it to the reading list in an introductory class and the discussion should be much livelier!

—**Dr. Hazel Morrow-Jones, associate professor, Department of City and Regional Planning, The Ohio State University**

"Our clients want to live in great places that they've never experienced before—a truly unique living space, not a suburban 'white box.' *Get Urban!* can help get them there.

—**Tammy Barrett, co-owner of the innovative NuStyle Development Company, Omaha, NE**

"Moving from the ex-urbs of Hampton Road to the 'Ghent' area of Norfolk was like moving to another world. A more fun and convenient world. *Get Urban!* helped us match our personality with the urban neighborhood we love!"

—**Timothy and Mindy Riley, a young, new city dweller couple who "got urban" in Norfolk, VA**

GET URBAN!

THE COMPLETE GUIDE TO CITY LIVING

GET URBAN!

THE COMPLETE GUIDE TO CITY LIVING

Kyle Ezell, AICP

CAPITAL
BOOKS, INC.
Sterling, Virginia

Capital Books, Inc.
P.O. Box 605
Herndon, Virginia 20172-0605

ISBN 1-931868-67-0 (alk.paper)

Library of Congress Cataloging-in-Publication Data

Ezell, Kyle.
  Get urban! : the complete guide to city living / Kyle Ezell.—1st ed.
    p.   cm.
    Includes index.
    ISBN 1-931868-67-0
    1. City and town life—United States.   2. Cities and towns—United States.
  3. City dwellers—United States. I. Title.

HT123.E94 2004
307.76'0973—dc22

                                                                    2003020953

Printed in the United States of America on acid-free paper that meets the American National Standards Institute Z39-48 Standard.

First Edition

10 9 8 7 6 5 4 3 2 1

Credits:

Book design: Susan Mark, Coghill Composition Company

Illustrations: Daniel Thomas, manager of Urban Design for the City of Columbus, Ohio's Planning Division

Photography: Kyle Ezell, except for photos taken in Jacksonville, Savannah, and Atlanta by Tim Young, AICP, uban planner for Columbia County, Georgia

Cover: Elsie Thomas and Stu Stull, creative consultants; Café Brioso, Downtown Columbus, Ohio

ACKNOWLEDGMENTS

Special thanks for the assistance given by the following people and organizations: Mary Martineau and the rest of the Short North Business Association, Columbus, Ohio; Sandy Wood, The Wood Companies, Columbus, Ohio; Bruce Dooley, owner of Dooley and Company Realtors, Columbus, Ohio; Shelley Scale, owner of Urban Living Properties in Austin, Texas; Mark Deutschmann, owner of Village Real Estate, Nashville, Tennessee; Robert W. Miller, owner of Monroe Properties, Richmond, Virginia; Bonnie Brehm in Columbus, Ohio, for use of her garden urb backyard; Tom Cooney, executive director of Forever Elmwood, Buffalo, New York; Don Scott and the Fort Worth South organization, Fort Worth, Texas; Kathleen Hughes, Capital Books' publisher for believing in this book's potential; Southwest Airlines for the cheap, safe, and reliable flights that took me around the country; Donna Hunter, administrator of the City of Columbus's Office of Land Management; Rich Sensenbrenner, Columbus City councilman; Chris Bender, director of communication, City of Washington, D.C., Office of Planning and Development; Robert Mick for all the inspiration; Gary Mann for "dessert rides" and for city talk for more than twenty years; Judy Coughlin; Mindy and Timothy Riley; Emily and Doug Stacey; Lindon, Glenda, Jennifer, and Andrew Ezell; Perky Myrick; Yvonne Gritzner; Carolyn and Brad Schwitters; Tara Montgomery; Jennifer Hughes; Dr. Hazel Morrow-Jones; Colleen Sims; R. C. Hoff; Charles Brewer; Rick Sawyer; Greg Haynes; Anne Wanner; Carson Combs; Holly Susong; Brian and Lisa Forchner; Mary Inbody and Marsha

Reichenbach; the Dale Lukens family; Tim Young for all your help and support; the Rose family in Knoxville, Tennessee; Jackie Newton; Tammy Barrett of NuStyle Companies, Omaha, Nebraska; Zoe Johnstone; Jim Bowen, River City Company, Chattanooga, Tennessee; Topher Finley; Jean Brodsky Bernard; Jim Hunter; and Lubina and Cliff Browning; Reza Reyazi, Elaine Hostetler, and Zubin Hostetler Reyazi; Beth Clark; Scott Poland; Kenneth Odom; Dan Irwin; Ronald Bonner; Doris Lyles; Martha Jo Gibbs; Sylvia Perry; John Bridger; Lamar and Ann Sitton; Karen Hundt; Holt Crowder; John Norwood; Gwynn Ware; Daphene Cope; Michael Wilcos and Theresa Brown.

And, most of all, thanks to Columbus, Ohio—my adopted city and my personal favorite in America. Your inspiring and superior urban neighborhoods caused me to begin this project and to enjoy my urban life every day.

CONTENTS

8 Considerations for Future Urbanites   209

This book is dedicated to my two fathers. First, to my biological father who raised me in Lawrenceburg, Tennessee, Ray Ezell. Thank you for sitting me down on your lap with a city atlas when I was five years old, accepting my lifelong geographic complex, and providing me with unconditional love. Second, to my academic father, Dr. Charles Gritzner, a distinguished professor of geography at South Dakota State University. How kind it was of you to take me under your wing, to share your love of geographic exploration. You taught me to think critically, to toil diligently, and never to give up on my dreams.

This book is also dedicated to three great women. First, to my academic mother, Dr. Priscilla Holland, geography professor at the University of North Alabama. If not for your interest and guidance, I would be completely, absolutely lost. Thanks for the direction and faith in my ability and magically setting me on course. To Ann Coulter at River City Company in Chattanooga, who taught me the valuable lesson— "Project what should be, not what is, and watch it come true." And to the coolest, most youthful, and truly special mother anyone could ever ask for, Glenda Ezell. You made me *everything* I am today, and I love you so much.

PREFACE

Why I Wrote This Book

While working for the City of Columbus, Ohio, I attended a mayoral ribbon-cutting ceremony for four new homes built in the Linden community, an inner city neighborhood about two miles northeast of the downtown. In an impassioned speech, the mayor of Columbus stated, "I invite you to come back, come back to Linden, rejoin the

community," as he pointed to the freshly constructed and still empty homes. That day, it occurred to me that Mayor Coleman was talking to suburbanites. They were the group that had long abandoned Linden for new cornfield subdivisions.

The Linden ribbon-cutting ceremony was a big deal. These new inner-city homes were heavily subsidized, were near a new transit station, and were built close to the sidewalk like the older surrounding neighborhood homes. The idea that the mayor and many other local officials, including even the television and newspaper media, were all making a hullabaloo out of four houses was compelling. Who would be moving there when hundreds of similar homes in newer outlying communities with better school systems were competing in the same real estate market? Suburbanites were targeted, but so were the local Lindenites who, if given the chance and opportunity, were ready to join the thousands of other Columbus locals who had fled to the new outlying communities.

Columbus is considered to be a healthy Midwestern city, but at the time of writing, it had around two thousand abandoned, vacant, and boarded-up properties in neighborhoods that have suffered huge population declines. One of my duties in that city job was selling old, abandoned structures in devastated areas to people willing to rehab the buildings, bring them up to building code, and then occupy them. Often, while I was standing on the crumbling front porches showing and selling the potential of the homes like a Realtor, many area residents expressed their hope that someone—anyone—would invest in their devastated neighborhoods, instead of buying new homes in nearby Ohio "ex-farms." Empty, decaying structures were cancer cells spreading quickly, killing what was otherwise a quality, historic urban neighborhood worth saving.

Columbus has good company. All over the United States, mayors' "state of the city" addresses stress revitalization of downtowns and surrounding neighborhoods. Elected and civic urban leaders obviously want people (namely, suburbanites) to choose an urban way of life over the normal and expected suburban lifestyle. Repopulating old neighborhoods, in fact, is now considered a matter of survival for many if not most cities.

This will only be successful when more people choose city life over suburbia. Even with the disturbing decline that has marked the recent history of most large American cities, many vibrant (and potentially vibrant) urban places remain. American cities are just beginning to market themselves in the same way suburban communities have been doing for years—as being great places to live. This book provides a showcase for such places.

Local newspapers are also beginning to feature return-to-the-city stories, encouraging people to consider what an urban lifestyle can offer. What all of these articles completely overlook is that returning to the city is not just a geographic move, it is also a transformation of mind-sets and expectations. Moving from suburbia to the city necessitates a major lifestyle transformation. This book is about understanding and achieving this kind of transformation.

The idea of a book that teaches suburbanites where to find and how to live an urban lifestyle might seem ludicrous. After all, suburban residents live only a short distance away from the urban parts of their regions. Many of them probably work in downtown offices and play at cultural, sport, and entertainment destinations. Suburbanites normally consider cities as places to hold jobs, dump their cars, have fun, and leave to return home as quickly as possible. This book offers a new way to view cities as they are intended to be viewed—for their full-time opportunities and benefits. Urban benefits are packaged here in an easy-to-understand format.

A lot of suburbanites may not be aware of the level of fun and convenience city life can bring. For them, walking to such things as shopping or entertainment is a totally alien concept. So is riding a bus. The same can be said for having the entire world outside one's front door. This book is beneficial because suburbanites, even those who probably would enjoy city life, have learned to avoid the city. They rarely visit the downtown and its surrounding neighborhoods unless such a trip is absolutely necessary. Using the principles outlined and described in this book will help get them out of their suburban shells.

It is important to note that although this is a pro-city book, it is written in a "suburban-neutral" tone. Although it assumes that readers are seeking a change, it also assumes that there is nothing wrong with suburban life. Living in the suburbs is a matter of choice and, in fact, it may be the correct choice for some families. The massive numbers of suburbanites who avoid the city, however, have caused a geographic void of knowledge about urban life. Very few people are familiar with cities, the way they work, what they look like, how they operate, and the exciting prospects they offer to residents. A lot of suburbanites have never been downtown in their lives.

This book stands out from the many others in that it does not bash suburban design or the suburban lifestyle. It would be counterproductive to suggest that the most common American dream is bad or unethical simply because everyday people want to enhance their lives by the promise of a serene suburban atmosphere. Suburbs have long been incubators for children whose parents insist on the highest-quality educational systems whose students almost always score overwhelmingly better in almost every category of education. Suburbs also are perceived as being safer and more "normal."

Unfortunately, most people today are suburban slaves, simply because they are imprisoned by the idea of living "as close to the city as possible to enjoy its benefits, but far enough away from the problems associated with city living." Even though suburbs may be pleasant enough, a growing number of people have begun to grow tired of the rather ordinary lives they offer. For a variety of personal reasons, they want a change. Some, for example, seek more excitement, increased mobility, and greater variety. This book provides a how-to manual directed toward those suburbanites who are willing to consider a completely new way of life.

As I began researching and writing this book, I consulted with many people, including city planners, college students, retirees, and other "average" individuals (including suburbanites). When told of the project's focus—presenting guidelines that will help suburbanites find and then move to downtown and inner-city neighborhoods—some people responded with concern and dismay: "You're writing a book about gentrification!" They said that encouraging suburbanites to move to the central city suggests advocating displacement of the poor by the incoming middle class (or worse—the rich!). Some said that the idea would encourage "monoculturation," or the homogenizing of an inner-city culture. According to them, suggesting, encouraging, and even helping suburbanites to become urbanites was simply the wrong thing to do.

As a "country boy" from very small-town rural America who has become a city lover of the highest order, I had a hard time believing that I was doing something wrong. To me, consciously advocating anything that would harm the city would be like hurting my mother or betraying a best friend. I moved to the city because I appreciate the convenience, the cultural opportunities, and the diversity of people, incomes, and ideologies. Traveling to more than fifty cities while conducting research for this book proved to me that most urban areas' physical and economic conditions are desperate for a population turnaround. New life for cities means including new people.

Since most cities have lost significant numbers of people, not advocating their growth means condoning their death. Discouraging development in the cities is counterproductive and, worse, irresponsible. A continuous flow of newcomers is needed to keep cities vibrant. Historically, these newcomers were foreign immigrants. Today, however, most immigrants skip the city entirely and head straight to the suburbs.

Despite what I consider to be the numerous important reasons for this book, the proliferation of concern and strong opinion from some members of my test group almost caused me to stop writing. I kept writing anyway—especially for places like Wichita; Peoria; Cincinnati; Pittsburgh; Birmingham; Tulsa; Des Moines; Jackson, Mississippi, and hundreds of other cities that can only hope for an "invasion" of urban pioneers.

Those American cities that lack the good fortune to be on the sunny coasts, the allure of Manhattan or San Francisco, and a booming economy or mountain view, can only survive if more people see the potential benefits of a city lifestyle. Legislating, overplanning, and condemning suburbs have not helped much.

Indeed, some high-demand cities with limited land have encountered negative effects from an onslaught of suburban-turned-urban residents. There is no disputing that some people have been displaced when their apartments are turned into upscale and expensive condominiums, or there is a steep and sudden increase in property values in now-popular neighborhoods. Some city neighborhoods also have turned into less funky places, replacing mom-and-pop stores with chain coffee shops. Even with cities dying slow, painful deaths, some consider gentrification to be worse than death itself.

The good news/bad news is that the overwhelming majority of America's heartland cities have suffered devastating population losses. Cities such as Cleveland, St. Louis, Detroit, and Philadelphia have each lost about 500,000 people in fifty years, while their suburbs' populations have swelled. Many others have declined almost as significantly. Growing cities like Nashville, Indianapolis, Louisville, Oklahoma City, and others have generally grown "on paper" because they have annexed huge tracts of suburban land, while many in-town neighborhoods continue to decline as fast as those in St. Louis and Detroit. Without question, there is plenty of room for spectacular urban regrowth in most of America.

This book is especially beneficial for those cities that are actively targeting the groups most likely to get urban: affluent and mobile baby boomers and fresh-faced, fickle twenty somethings. Over the last few decades, cities have tried hard to bring these people (and anyone else) back to town. They've built palatial stadiums and convention centers that feature spectacular architecture, organized fireworks shows on every Fourth of July, and held elaborate cultural festivals. They've put up banners that read, "Live-Work-Play-Shop," on the main streets to lure suburbanites to the urban life. A lot of cities experiencing "brain drain" are trying to attract young, creative people such as artists and technology whizzes to bring new life to their dead cores. I believe that all of these individual strategies are important (especially the last one), but a more comprehensive, sustainable, and long-term approach must accompany them: an urban lifestyle education.

Tomorrow's most sought-after cities will not be those on the latest "hot city" list, but those that are genuinely cool because of the quality, authentic urban lifestyles they offer. For this to happen, cities must get back to the basics of improving deteriorating infrastructures, refurbishing older landmark buildings, providing great parks and entertainment opportunities, and, most of all, building *a lot* of houses for people of all incomes. Cities that offer their residents easy access to food and everyday goods, interesting ways to move around, amusement waiting outside their doors, safe well-lit streets, and numerous opportunities for spontaneous human interaction are those that locals become more attached to and others will flock to.

Cities at the top of their growth and economic development game will have the greatest number of satisfied "customers" of all ages, in-comes, races, backgrounds, and cultures who not only can sustain themselves in downtown and its surrounding neighborhoods, but thrive there as well. I'm not naïve enough to believe that suburbanites who change their minds will save American downtowns by them-selves, but I strongly believe that cities with the largest number of res-idents who are aware of the tremendous benefits of real urban living will be able to provide more city living opportunities. Those cities that offer the most interesting urban places to call home, and offer them first, will quickly become the most sought-after destinations for thou-sands of eager newcomers.

Actively encouraging (especially teaching) people how to move to and live in America's cities introduces a new level of awareness. This kind of awareness will create dialogue, prompting city neighborhoods to anticipate and then prepare for a successful integration of new resi-dents. Readers of this manual who actually move to cities will know what to expect, what to contribute, and what to fight for—a place for everyone to live together.

Get Urban! should be considered a work of urban anthropology and geography (the author's fields of academic study)—a primer for the would-be urbanite. It is important to understand that it is *not* a travel guide. There are no specific addresses for good restaurants or tourist destinations. This book offers a remedial lesson in urban living. It is about the feelings evoked by living in the city, the personalities of ur-ban neighborhoods, and the many wonderful opportunities that city dwellers can enjoy.

Now that this book is finished, I plan to work on a series of *Return-to-the-City Guides* that will feature dozens of urban neighborhoods that want to repopulate. These books will have a much more detailed account of specific destinations such as hangouts, special restau-rants, places to live and rent, and costs of living. They will also in-clude local expectations about how urban neighborhoods view themselves, how they want to grow, and the local flavor they want to retain. The books will feature fundamental strategies for attracting new-comers and keeping locals as well—everyone's goal for a truly success-ful urban renaissance.

It is my hope that my love and enthusiasm for cities will be evident in the chapters that follow. Urban life, relatively unknown and hidden in plain sight of the sprawling suburbs, can be a fulfilling, exciting, and fun experience. I know, because this book is written from personal experience. I now live and thoroughly enjoy the environment about which this book is written.

I invite you to begin perhaps your life's most important journey—GET URBAN!

1

Are You Ready for a Life Adventure?

Are you tired of any of the following?

- Cutting grass
- Commuting
- Driving everywhere for everything
- Taking care of a needy house
- Being a long way from entertainment, unique shopping, and work

Are you longing for . . .

- A home in a special neighborhood that has character and personality
- More close relationships with people who live nearby
- More convenience in your life
- A close connection with a special place
- Easy and immediate access to shopping and fun

Are you ready to . . .

- Engage with a diverse group of people
- Simplify your home living so you can be out of the house more
- Park your car once and for all

- Walk to restaurants, theaters, bookstores, sports arenas, and art galleries
- Say good-bye to boredom

Imagine living in a place that offers countless and exciting opportunities to engage life, where walking on electric sidewalks, shopping at special stores, and eating at extraordinary restaurants is common. Sipping coffee on a lively sidewalk patio and catching up with friends is part of a normal day. Imagine making new friends with interesting and varied backgrounds and ethnicities and meeting them at an outdoor food festival or joining in a rally in the park for an important cause. Picture a carefree dog walk in the morning, followed by volunteering in the community in the evening. Think of the kind of bustle that is produced by people living with inexhaustible energy on busy streets. Now imagine all of this (and more) happening within close proximity to your home.

Home could be an apartment that was previously an abandoned factory building or a historic structure with ornate trim and handsome architecture. Or it could be a few rooms above a storefront where you can watch the world go by on the sidewalk below. Home could also be a row house with a limestone stoop, where neighbors gossip and kids play. Or it could be a new high-rise condominium with a spectacular view of the city skyline. In any case, home would offer a neighborhood that could never be described as being boring.

This kind of life could provide an energy-filled existence full of choices to stimulate the mind and spirit. Just steps away, dancing at a pulsating nightclub or retreating to a sedate bookstore can be choices, depending on your mood. Walking to a mom-and-pop diner today, then to a five-star bistro tomorrow is possible. Joining a gym, attending church, enrolling in karate or art classes (or both), playing piano at a local bar, joining a book club, rollerblading, and any other activities could await you just outside the front door. Get energized on a whim or become anonymous in a crowd. Participate in a cultural festival or watch people on a park bench.

So much is possible for city dwellers. Cities offer their residents the kind of electric lifestyle that comes from urban energy. Most of all, cities can offer endless possibilities for personal growth and never having to use the excuse, "There's nothing to do," again.

This kind of lifestyle is not for everyone, but it could be for you. If you are someone who thrives on everyday variety and excitement, city life may be just as exhilarating as a jungle safari, downhill skiing, or sky-diving is to "normal" people.

This is a guide to transforming lifestyles for people who want to undergo a geographic and personal metamorphosis. People who will get the most out of this book are those who live in the suburbs near a city or in disconnected subdivisions (in or near any size town) that are tucked away from the world. Following the lessons below, readers will experience a dramatic change from a restless and isolated suburbanite into an activity junkie and connected urbanite. If you are reading this book, you're probably somewhat unhappy with your life in the suburbs. More likely, you're just bored. This book will lead you on a personal quest to find the kind of urban environment in which you can thoroughly enjoy living.

The quest to relocate to such a place can be a most fulfilling journey. Before settling in a city, however, you must undertake a considerable amount of thought and planning. As an introduction to the process of finding and moving to a quality urban place, understanding your current "normal" living situation is essential.

NORMAL SUBURBIA

Generally speaking, the American way of life is not an urban way of life. Living in an urban environment is not considered by many to be "normal." This is evidenced by a popular marketing catchphrase used in most city downtowns and in-town neighborhoods across the country—"Live. Work. Play. Shop." The four words mean just what they say, and urban boosters use them on banners and brochures to lure the masses out of malls, drive-through windows, and freeways and into the city to practice these four daily activities in urban neighborhoods. The concept of having a home, a job, fun, and everyday goods—most of our daily needs—within close proximity to each other, is radical. After all, the common American dream includes wide-open spaces, big backyards, and multicar garages—all of which have nothing to do with cities.

Even though the live-work-play-shop phrase has been around for several years, it still is aimed at, and drilled into, suburbanites. This slogan argues that cities are indeed worth considering for what has come to be an attractive alternative lifestyle choice. The campaign has had varying degrees of success: urban residence and lifestyle remain a distant and vague anomaly in the minds and experience of most people living in the United States.

Outside the U.S., living in cities is not considered to be odd at all. Throughout much of the rest of the world, in fact, urban life is expected, "normal," and desired. Cities such as London, Amsterdam, Paris, Hong Kong, Singapore, Zurich, Copenhagen, Buenos Aires, and countless others offer ample proof of the residential attractiveness of city living. In many cities, including those of South America and Canada, the most desirable places to live are as close to the city center as possible. Most of the world's people equate urban living with having easy access to culture, endless entertainment, and everyday conveniences. You will never see street banners in central London or Stockholm that beg people to live, work, play, and shop—they already do.

Since the dawn of the urban era, thousands of years ago, living in cities has been considered the normal thing to do. Ancient cities such as Rome, Athens, Cairo, and many others have been around for millennia. In the Americas, the Inca built grand cities, including the magnificent Machu Picchu. In Mexico, the cities of Tenochtitlán and Teotihuacán rivaled Old World urban centers in both size and splendor. Only in recent history has city living begun to decline—and that decline has largely been influenced by American settlement patterns.

From the mid-1800s until the end of World War II, American cities thrived. They bustled with the kind of old-world activity found in London and Rome. In addition to New York, Boston, Philadelphia, and Chicago, the big, important places were cities such as St. Louis, Detroit, New Orleans, Pittsburgh, and Cleveland. Unfortunately, the negative effects of the industrial revolution—including smoke, dust, odors, water pollution, and excessive noise—were directly associated with these embryonic cities. So were such realities as overcrowding, poor sanitary conditions, deplorable working conditions, and, often, poverty.

The desirable aspects of city life, however, came hand-in-hand with the negative ones. There were busy commercial streets teeming with business, lively sidewalk traffic, and strong, vital downtowns. Until the mid-twentieth century, many American cities equaled or exceeded the pace of older cities in Europe and Asia. But, even then, urban life quality often was quite poor. When trolley lines allowed people to live a few miles away from the filth and commotion, those who could afford the move quickly fled the cities. The idea of large-scale suburban living (largely an American innovation) was born. New outlying communities burgeoned due to such social factors as poor race relations (desegregation during the middle 1900s caused "white flight" to the suburbs) and a new, widely held idea that the rich and privileged should live in the country, but still within easy reach of the city.

Indeed, millions of Americans live close to, but not in, cities. These places have become known as suburbs. Since the mid-1940s, when members of the "Greatest Generation" survived World War II and moved to Levittown, New York's prototype cookie-cutter subdivisions, suburban living has become the desired and expected way of life for most of us. Millions of people fled the inner cities for their little plot of land complete with a new tract home and a big backyard. Most baby boomers and Generation Xers have lived their entire lives in suburban communities, and there is every reason to believe that the majority of young people today will follow their predecessors farther out from the inner city.

The term, "American dream," has come to mean living close enough to the city to enjoy its cultural amenities, but far enough away to avoid its problems. People who actually choose to live in the city are looked on as being abnormal, unusual, and even foolish. Years of suburban living have trained Americans to avoid the city most of the time, only venturing into the urban environment to sample a taste of city life when an urban fix is needed. A retreat to the solitude of the cul-de-sac and quiet neighborhood is considered to be a reward. For some, however, it is banishment to a wretchedly dull life.

Indeed, suburbs often provide an excellent quality of life. Their relative peace, perceived safety from crime, and good schools helped these residential areas to market easy sales pitches for suburban community boosters. Suburbs have come to be viewed as "escapelands," places to flee the problems of the city. For seven decades, people (who were able) quickly abandoned the cities (considered "bad" and dangerous places) for "good," safe suburban havens.

Suburban living is often described in terms of what it does not have—

a place to avoid people who are not "like you" for neighbors; a place with lower levels of indiscriminate crime; a place without high-rise buildings, old houses, and abandoned structures. The list of "doesn't haves" goes on and on. Suburbs have been the target destination for people who want to escape urban ills, and their descriptions are as numerous as are their reasons to escape. Americans have voted with their feet and suburbia has won: "normal" means life in suburbia.

"Weird," Exciting Urbia

Generally speaking, people in America are not supposed to live in cities. Most people want quiet, peaceful places where they can hide from the world. With so much available countryside for building houses, what can be said of people who seek out pulsating, exciting, diverse places to live? They may have traveled to Vancouver or Barcelona and recall the exhilaration they experienced when visiting a great urban center. Now, they are drawn to a similar lifestyle in a full-time, homegrown urban environment.

Readers who will benefit most from this book are those who enjoy varied activities, spontaneity, and numerous lifestyle opportunities, and who sincerely want to live in an enjoyable urban atmosphere (in other words, "weirdos"). "Weirdo" is the perfect word to describe a person who is disenchanted with a community that provides residents with everything they need and what most people want—a roof overhead, safe streets, shopping malls, and good schools.

It is also weird to want to relocate in the reverse direction of contemporary migration. Suburban values and "roots" are powerful. To defy the normal patterns of society, including perhaps family and friends, can seem bizarre. In other words, choosing to move where most people have been fleeing for decades is probably considered to be strange.

Today, regardless of age, most Americans have spent most of their lives in the suburbs. Besides ignoring the benefits of quiet subdivision streets and privacy, those who want a city lifestyle are rejecting the primary landscape associated with being "American." After all, this is not Europe or South America. Aspiring to live in the city is, indeed, weird.

For perhaps the first time in American history, city living, although still considered to be abnormal by many people, has finally become desirable—as places where many people *choose* to live. Americans are just beginning to see the great potential and many exhilarating possibilities that urban living can offer. City life could (and should) become normal again.

The Ready and Willing Urban Migrant

In addition to the general suburban population, this book targets people who are most likely to "get urban," like the groundswell of baby boomers who are ready to retire. Around seventy-eight million baby boomers are entering their postproductive years, and many have "empty nests." They plan to stay active and generally disdain cloistered retirement homes. Baby boomers want to retire to exciting, engaging, and fun-filled neighborhoods. Most baby boomers have lived their entire lives in the suburbs, and this book offers a quick course in urban geography that can help them find their desired city home.

The book is also aimed at young people who are ready to start out in adult life, but who were incubated in suburbs. Many of them, especially college graduates, are seeking fun *Friends* lifestyles instead of strip malls. Young people's energy and creativity call for an urban, rather than suburban, way of life. They will find useful lessons in the following chapters.

Retiring baby boomers can probably choose to live anywhere; young people are concerned primarily with establishing their careers. Choosing a city, and especially an urban neighborhood where they can thrive, *and then* finding a job is a healthy way to approach life. Being stuck in an out-of-the-way suburb or in a city that doesn't meet their personal needs means sacrificing a well-rounded (and more fun) lifestyle. After all, quality nights and weekends should matter at least as much as workdays. Thoughtfully considering what they want out of a place should come first, and this book will help in their search for an individualized urban life.

Both of these groups tend to focus on distant or unattainable neighborhoods (such as those in Manhattan or San Francisco), and they are generally unaware that overlooked cities (even their own hometowns) offer urban lifestyles identical to those found in more famous neighborhoods and larger cities. This book demonstrates that *any* city can offer near-identical experiences to those found in better-known places.

CHANGING YOUR VALUES SYSTEMS

It seems almost ridiculous that people living so close to the city, even working downtown during the day and attending cultural events at night, would need help finding and then moving to the city. After all, their homes are often just a short drive down the freeway. Suburbs are often considered extensions of the greater city, but life there could not be more different. The move from the suburbs to the city is much more than a geographic change: it requires an entirely new mental outlook— even a complete reversal of core personal values.

This change of values is not of the religious or moral variety. Rather, it is a change in values pertaining to what you do, whom you do it with, where and how you spend time, and how the days' events will play out. For instance, walking to work instead of driving may seem bizarre. Driving everywhere has been a long-standing suburban value. Many city dwellers value walking and would never consider driving to work, the store, or other proximate locations. Likewise, the entrenched suburban value of living in widely spaced single-family homes with plenty of room to spread out to enjoy an abundance of privacy and independence is difficult to shake. Urban values require living in high-density neighborhoods, sharing space with many others in a small area.

Another suburban value is having a desire for things "new" and "clean," including houses, streets, neighborhoods, churches, and stores. When cities get old and dirty, most suburbanites relocate to newer and cleaner communities, often even farther away from the city. Urbanites value things that are old and full of history. Neighborhood memoirs, gritty streets, and distinctive character are important city values. Determining where to move is important, but tweaking entrenched suburban values systems is equally critical.

Development values, those that govern how people feel about construction and population growth, must change as well when moving to the city. For instance, suburbanites fret over proposed subdivisions bringing new homes and people who will surely clog roads, overcrowd the school system, and destroy back porch views. On the other hand, urbanites cheer on hearing news of "infill" development that promises more people, business, and vitality. Suburbanites place high value on cul-de-sac lots in tucked-away subdivisions that allow them to hide away from the world, so they want to restrict further growth immediately after they arrive. Urbanites value residential buildings in the middle of the city's activity and action and appreciate new buildings, full of new people, that are built on former parking lots. These are only a couple of examples. It is critical that these fundamentally opposite viewpoints and values are understood before blindly relocating to the city. This book is a vehicle for evaluating these different outlooks.

Even for people on the fence, who are merely considering a city move, this book will help them to imagine living in a real city with opportunities and experiences that are not available in the suburbs. It will prompt readers to envision specific events, situations, and circumstances that urban life could contribute to their lives. Perhaps you can see yourself with season tickets to the symphony or making your way down a sidewalk bursting at the seams with activity while on the way to a hopping nightclub. Maybe frequenting an Asian teahouse filled with an eclectic cast of characters is in your future. If "being yourself" is important, personal expression in dress, culture, and ideology may be key. Meeting other urbanites with varied backgrounds and interesting perspectives may be what you desire. Only you know what "getting urban" means in terms of what it can contribute to your enjoyment of life. Perusing the lessons found in this book will help solidify your goals.

URBAN DRAWS AND SUBURBAN FLAWS

Some people have lived their entire lives in suburbs, but they have never fully integrated into the suburban environment. Their personalities do not match their home landscapes. If this sounds like you, you need to understand the specific reasons why you feel this way and what you want to change. For instance, for history buffs who appreciate a mix of architecture surrounded by a creative atmosphere, a typical subdivision might seem stifling and incongruent with "who they are." Some people feel like prisoners of oversized lawns, upset by the high water bills required to keep their grass as green as the neighbors'. Traffic jams and relying totally on automobiles—and, especially, experiencing the strange phenomenon of being stuck in a traffic jam on what was recently a country road—might fill some people with dread.

You probably know you belong in the city, or you wouldn't be reading this book. However, just saying you want to move to the city isn't enough. If you're seriously considering a change from suburbanite to urban dweller, you need to understand exactly what that means and involves personally. What specific aspects are drawing you into the city?

Pinpointing the specific kinds of city amenities you seek can help to focus the search. Knowing where, how, and why these things are important will point you in the right direction to the right location. Before proceeding further, read the following worksheet and take the time to think about the positive aspects of the city and your specific reasons for wanting to move there. Keep in mind that these examples are primers for brainstorming your own urban "draw factors."

YOUR "URBAN DRAWS" WORKSHEET

List as many things as you can that are "drawing" you into the city. What is it about a city lifestyle that you find appealing? Explain each in as much detail as possible (and feel free to use extra space on additional paper). This will help you to determine the kind of urban environment that is right for you.

ENTERTAINMENT:

What activities would city life provide that the suburbs cannot?

_____

_____

_____

_____

What kinds of new hobbies would you undertake if you lived in the city?

_____

_____

_____

_____

If you moved to the city, what would be an ordinary night for you?

_____

_____

_____

_____

Describe an extraordinary weekend full of activities of your choosing.

_____

_____

_____

_____

Explain how living closer to these activities would change your life.

_____

_____

_____

_____

ECOLOGY:

List any particular natural environment issues that would be enhanced or affected by a move to the city.

_____

_____

_____

_____

LIFESTYLE:

What does the term "urban lifestyle" mean to you?

_____

_____

_____

_____

Explain why a city move would allow you to realize this kind of life.

_____

_____

_____

_____

HEALTH:

Would you anticipate any healthy benefits of moving to the city? If so, what kinds?

_____

_____

_____

_____

MOBILITY:

How will you get around differently in the city, and how will this be an improvement?

_____

_____

_____

_____

POLITICS:

Do you have any political reasons for moving to the city?

_____

_____

_____

_____

SENSE OF PLACE:

What elements of a place make you feel at home?

_____

_____

_____

_____

NEED FOR ADVENTURE:

What is it about the city that makes your adrenaline rush?

_____

_____

_____

_____

How would a city life satisfy your adventurous side?

_____

_____

_____

_____

HOUSING:

What kind of urban structure can you see yourself living in?

_____

_____

_____

_____

How is this living space different from your suburban home? List any advantages.

_____

_____

_____

_____

PEOPLE:

What kinds of people do you want to spend your day with in the city?

_____

_____

_____

_____

Is this different from what you can experience in suburbia? How?

_____

_____

_____

_____

YOUR "SUBURBAN FLAWS" WORKSHEET

What aspects of your life in the suburbs are getting on your nerves? Using this sheet will help you think about and then solidify personal reasons why your suburban home just shouldn't be "home" anymore.

Describe your biggest suburban irritant in detail here.

_____

_____

_____

_____

What other suburban lifestyle issues are making you consider a move to the city?

1. _____

_____

_____

_____

2. _____

_____

_____

_____

3. _____

_____

_____

_____

4. _____

_____

_____

_____

Knowing what you want is important, but it is just as important to determine what aspects of your current suburban living environment you consider to be flawed, aspects that are "pushing" you away from the suburbs. Writing down your "suburban flaws" will help you critically assess what you should avoid to achieve your desired urban lifestyle. Only you know the reasons for your discontent.

LET THE TRANSFORMATION BEGIN

Now you should understand the kind of living environment and lifestyle you're seeking as well as the kind you're fleeing. You've taken the first important step toward moving to the city. For the journey to end in a quality urban environment that will meet your needs and your personality requires much thought and reflection. The rest of this book will lead you toward a quality urban environment that matches your personality, interest, and pocketbook. You'll learn what kind of place to look for, where to begin looking for it, and how to undertake the search. Specifically, chapter 2 features "The Urban Quality Checklist," which introduces ten universal elements found in a quality urban environment. Understanding the basic principles in the Urban Quality Checklist provides the background information and perspectives needed to critically analyze an urban living environment. Chapter 3 offers a simple step-by-step geography lesson that assists readers in knowing where to look for a quality urban environment. The concept of an "urb" (a place with opposite lifestyle characteristics from suburbs) is introduced here as the target destination.

Chapters 4 through 7 help the reader match specific kinds of urban environments to his or her personality. Four types of urban settings offer their own unique ambience, housing choices, and other opportunities. By determining which type of urban environment matches their wants, needs, and personalities, readers can find their ideal urban experience in any city. Because many people spend more time thinking about which outfit to wear than where they live, chapter 8 prepares suburbanites for their upcoming life adventure. You will learn urban survival skills, including searching for a city home, "schlepping," dealing with your fear of crime, preparing for unique urban weather conditions, blending into your new neighborhood, and learning how to walk again.

Let's get started!

2

THE URBAN QUALITY CHECKLIST

Ten universal elements to look for in a quality urban environment

Finding a quality urban environment is not something that can be quantified perfectly or looked up. The study of cities is a social science, and like all other social sciences, statistically analyzing soft ideas (the feeling evoked from a crowded city sidewalk stroll or the way the sun's rays bounce off the downtown skyline at a certain time of day) is ridiculous. In the same way, the search for a quality urban lifestyle means different things to different people. This process requires soul searching, marked by experiencing and personally evaluating prospective urban places. In other words, it requires work.

Without offering a hard and fast formula, this chapter guides your search for the right kind of city environment for you. Called the "Urban Quality Checklist," it contains universal elements found in every quality urban environment. Any method claiming to be "universal" (like this one) should be used with caution. Think of it as a self-help list, a guide to assist in a life journey. The Urban Quality Checklist encourages you to think of personal examples and apply them to urban experiences, memory, and perceptions. It should be used like a cookbook—stick with the basic recipe but add spices and other special ingredients to suit personal tastes.

Understanding the basic principles in the Urban Quality Checklist provides the background information and perspective needed to analyze an urban living environment. The list is intended to be taken with you as you search for "home." It is an evaluation sheet that allows prospective urbanites to apply each item to their individual real-world experience. The list below summarizes each element of the urban quality evaluation process in some detail and is followed by a fictitious scenario that helps to condition and stimulate the urbanite in everyone. When the time comes to set off on the actual journey in search of a city home, knowing the principles in this section will help suburbanites in their search for a suitable urban environment to recognize a quality city "when they see it."

1 . Choose a Close-in Urban Location

The first step in becoming an urbanite involves mental reconditioning. For decades, suburbanites have been conditioned to avoid inner cities (because they are "bad, scary places"). Their scope is limited to those places that provide all the benefits of the city without having to deal with the problems of the city. Those kinds of places are suburbs. The reconditioning process begins with focusing the geographic scope on the downtown proper and its immediate surrounding area. In the search for a quality urban lifestyle, center cities must be the target destination—even with all of their associated problems.

Choosing to live in the center city is the most basic item on the urban quality checklist—the foundation on which all of the other items build. It is the most urban section, the place that looks and feels most like a city because it actually is a city. Naturally (at least for urbanites), the core city has the most to offer. As foreign as this close-in location might seem to the majority of suburbanites, there are many good reasons for moving there.

The center city is special because it is built on a historic street plan. Streets here were planned by local founders who toiled over the details that would determine how their future city would function and look. As is covered in the next chapter, living on the original street plan means truly living in the city.

Central city streets (unlike those in the suburbs) try to link everything to everything else. They allow pedestrians to get around with ease. City streets also allow cars to move from point A to point B in many ways. In most American cities, the farther your home is from the downtown, the more complicated it is to move around. For instance, the route from a suburban cul-de-sac to a shopping center can often be as tangled as the maze confronting a laboratory mouse.

The center city features the greatest presentation of timeless architecture. Government buildings anchor important intersections and display magnificent features such as carved masonry, tall pillars or columns, gargoyles, and grand entrances. The oldest churches are often built in the city center by residents who wanted to mimic the beautiful structures in their countries of origin. Stately old department stores still stand in many cities, remaining irreplaceable even if their original retail functions have long been abandoned. One-hundred-year-old office buildings display ornate architectural details. The farther away you are from the middle of the city, the less likely you are to find such detailed, impressive urban structures.

Longevity and history are two other good reasons to focus on the middle of the city. Downtowns and surrounding neighborhoods were built to last. Old, even abandoned industrial buildings in the inner city have enduring strength and distinctive beauty. Historic inner-city residential neighborhoods were built for future generations. Regardless of a neighborhood's condition, most are still filled with historical architecture and leafy, mature trees that line long-established streets. This is why the best urban neighborhood parks also share a close-in address.

City views are best in and around the downtown area. Having skyline vistas (especially close enough to be able to make out building details) underscores city living. Whether from a window, rooftop, street, or over the trees, city people appreciate city views.

The most important reason to locate close in is because it's fun. Downtown is normally home to such cultural institutions as museums, live-performance theaters, opera houses, and symphony halls. Less highbrow venues, such as mom-and-pop restaurants, sports facilities, corner bars, unusual sidewalk cafés, and the most celebrated restaurants are all there (or soon will be). Outdoor farmers' markets, urban walking and bike trails along riverfronts, and alternative shopping experiences provide fun opportunities for city people.

Living the Inward Lifestyle

The sky turns to dusk on a Friday evening as you sit in the living room inside a tenth-floor loft apartment. Sharing space on the couch with Friday-night-out clothes, you decide to get up and open the blinds. The entire city is beginning to change priorities from work to play. This view is one of life's simple urban pleasures. The end of rush hour below coincides with dinnertime. Deciding to eat on the sofa was a good idea—the city view is spectacular tonight. As dusk gives way to darkness, the lights turn the city into an urban night's dawn. It's time to get ready to meet your friends who will be waiting a block away at the bookstore café. Another block down the street, your favorite restaurant and bar has a table for five reserved. At the end of that same block (at the concert hall) is where you'll meet your blind date. On the way out of your apartment, you realize how much you appreciate this fun-filled urban lifestyle.

The bottom line is—if you're moving to the city, do it right—actually move to *the city*.

2. POSITION YOURSELF

Few things are more luxurious than being able to walk to places to shop and have interesting experiences. When searching for an ideal urban living environment, pay special attention to places that provide ready access to employment, entertainment, school (if needed), doctors, retail and food, and other personal necessities for the good life. The possibility of walking to both fun and functional destinations is an almost exclusively urban characteristic. It also makes residents feel attached to their neighborhoods because their lives are truly local. The ability to be an anytime pedestrian means that city homes become everything and everyone in the greater neighborhood.

When "culture vultures" can walk a few blocks to their weekly show or play, favorite art gallery, or concert hall—instead of driving miles and scavenging for a parking space—their lives are enhanced. Health buffs who can jog to the gym or take a bicycle to a health store combine functional routines with exercise. Workaholics who live just steps from the office can work longer hours. Park enthusiasts with space for their dogs to run and a seasonal ice-skating rink as an extension of their front porch think they live in heaven. Having a local city environment that matches your individual personality means being correctly "positioned" in your urban neighborhood.

The most important positioning is near food. Living within walking distance of places to find food—both restaurants and groceries—should be a top priority. The most attractive, sought-after areas already have full-service grocery stores, outdoor public markets, street vendors, and/or pedestrian-oriented convenience stores. If an urban neighborhood has this kind of food selection, it is truly a quality place to live. A nearby food source saves time and frustration, because if sustenance must be found somewhere, it might as well be a short walk away.

A positioned lifestyle is also called living in a "mixed-use" environment. "Mixed use" is a term used mostly by urban planners to describe a lot of different kinds of services and land uses (such as businesses, medical offices, workplaces, houses, restaurants, shops, etc.) located together in a small area. Life in suburbia usually provides the opposite pattern. The grocery store, restaurants, and retail stores were built in different locations far away from houses in closed-off subdivisions. Urban places with a variety of mixed uses supply the kinds of goods and services that local pedestrians need daily—and like having close by.

Another important consideration is being located near public transportation routes. Public transportation in most of suburbia is either an afterthought or unavailable. Urbanites find it a shame when the train station or bus or trolley stop is too far away from home. Other than the great convenience and the time and money savings that public transportation offers, having access nearby provides alternatives when city streets are blocked. Special events such as parades and festivals, more common conditions like traffic jams, and regional draws like sporting events or concerts slow traffic and create parking problems. Snowstorms or heavy rain makes the bus or train seem more practical—even more desirable—than driving. Especially during such times (in fact, anytime!), being located near a bus or train becomes a luxury.

Being positioned correctly requires thinking about everything that makes the urban experience more functional, enjoyable, and "urban." Having easy access to as many experiences as possible should be a pri-

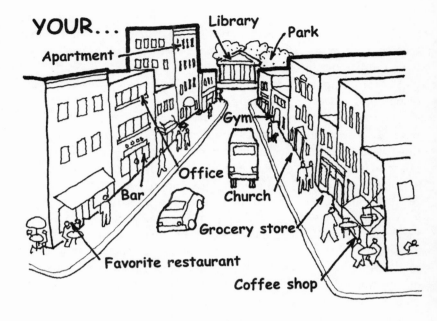

mary goal. Enjoying an urban location near hobbies, shopping, working, playing, and getting around ensures quality urban living.

3. Seek Out "Mallternatives"

Special corridors lined with businesses that feature interesting and, sometimes, alternative retail stores are called "mallternatives." They provide a much different shopping experience from a conventional suburban shopping mall and usually specialize in nontraditional merchandise. Mallternatives have become such a highly attractive and unique shopping experience that even suburbanites use them as much as urban locals.

Mallternatives act like old-fashioned Main Streets with their clusters of retail businesses. Shopping choices here are varied. Secondhand clothing stores, luxury restaurants, bologna and cheese shops, antiques rows, bookstores, and modern art galleries are all common. Pedestrians gaze at

Successful Positioning

It's a weekday morning. Still groggy and in your pajamas, you slip on comfortable slippers, throw on an overcoat and a cap, and stumble down the stairs out onto the sidewalk. A block down the street, at your favorite twenty-four-hour diner, several of your neighbors have saved a seat for you. One friend laughingly greets you with a still-hot cup of coffee with milk and two packets of sugar: "Wake up, sleepyhead!" The banana nut muffin is good, as is catching up with friends—but it's time to get ready for work.

Fully awake now, you buy a newspaper at the convenience store on the walk back home and talk to a neighbor who is taking a break from walking her dog. At home, you down the last warm sip of coffee and scan the paper. Your partner steps out of the shower just in time for your uninterrupted morning routine.

It gets interrupted anyway. A thunderclap jolts the building—rain has started falling suddenly in sheets. No problem. Your oversize umbrella and raincoat is all that is necessary to make it the half-block to the bus stop. The bus arrives five minutes later and drops you off at the office door with fifteen minutes to spare. The sun comes out during lunch hour, a great chance to run errands on foot—the post office, the bank, and a quick haircut, all in an hour. On the bus ride home, you decide to pick up something fresh for dinner, which means getting off at the grocery store about three blocks from home.

Pasta, fresh veggies, wine, and bread fit into your canvas shoulder bag, allowing for an easy schlep. The three-block walk home is easy, yet difficult—there are too many distractions. The drugstore is having a sale on exactly the items you need. The local theater is selling tickets for Saturday night's debut. The gym, easily visible in the windows overhead, is full of people on stationary bicycles—a personal reminder to join them after dinner. Then you remember your friend who is playing guitar on the outdoor patio café in the park tonight. It's on the calendar, and a promise is a promise. It occurs to you that you haven't left your neighborhood in over a month. Then you think, "What would be the point?"

the windows. People eat at tables on the sidewalk. Spontaneous encounters happen here because mallternatives are where people celebrate urban life.

Mallternatives are often considered to be the primary location that defines the neighborhood. Urbanites love them because they provide opportunities to be around other interesting people in a festive urban

Broughton Street in Savannah has transformed quickly into a spectacular mallternative.

atmosphere. This atmosphere causes some people to consider them to be trendy and refer to them as "boutique rows." In reality, stores here may be no more trendy than those found in suburban malls. It is the urban experience, not necessarily the stores, that makes them special places. Perhaps special is trendy.

Mallternatives are unusual because the kinds of activities that happen on their streets and sidewalks cannot be duplicated in any indoor mega shopping center or strip mall. Simply walking down the sidewalk is everyday fun. They also hold social events such as "Gallery Hops," "Music in the City," or other scheduled activities outdoors and centered on pedestrians.

Contrary to the name, mallternatives do not try to be malls or to compete with malls. They provide an ambience for urbanites who may be less interested in shopping than in experiencing city life. Mallternative corridors stimulate visitors with funky colors, unusual scenes, and

The awesome High Street mallternative, Columbus, Ohio.

places to gather and "people watch." They are almost always chosen as parade routes because they are charged with urban electricity.

Mallternatives can even have chain stores like Starbucks and McDonald's as long as they blend in with all kinds of other businesses. Unless the entire area is invaded by chains, the presence of a few chain businesses cannot eliminate the out-of-the-ordinary ambience provided by a minigrocery store, a local bookstore, and a pot-smokers' head shop. Any mixture of unusual and more common stores attracts a mix of people and makes browsing an enjoyable experience. Good urban design also adds to the magic.

4. Look for Active Sidewalks and Streets

Suburban people typically seek quiet subdivisions with more trees than people. Moving to the city requires a completely different mind-set—lots of pedestrians on the sidewalks is considered a good thing. Urban

---

Your Mallternative—Better than Television

After several hours of sitting outside at a sidewalk café watching people, you notice that your local mallternative is so many things to so many people. Art lovers consider it their gallery row as they enthuse over the featured artist's sculptures. Suburbanites use it as a stylish place where they can be pampered—the place to get a facial or have their nails or hair done. Teenagers make it the place to take their first dates for a stroll. Traditional indoor mall walkers come here to walk outside, huffing and puffing with their hand weights. The street vendor hawks hot dogs and pretzels and they sell like crazy on this sunny day. The local bar attracts a wonderful mix of old-timers, purple-haired "freaks," and all kinds of friends. Then you realize that this is your place, your soul's home—your mallternative.

---

places with no people are "ghost towns." City lovers aren't moving to the city to live in a ghost town.

Quality city life means vibrant sidewalks full of busy people. Living on or near an active city street makes the day seem like an evolving movie script. Different characters appear and disappear, adding to a constantly shifting plot. It's hard to be bored on an active city street—a new "live movie" is featured every day.

Constantly changing city moods also eliminate apathy. Good and bad news generated by important world events is often evident on the faces of people sharing the sidewalk. Excitement over an upcoming street festival brings a mood of anticipation, evidenced by merchants scurrying to meet opening deadlines or wide-eyed children anxious to reach their destinations.

Sidewalks act as the city's nervous system. They reflect the mad rush hour's stress, a jovial lunch break in the park, a high-energy night on the town. Sidewalks also display a kind of organized chaos that most city people expect to make them feel like they're home.

Active streets are generally safer than empty streets simply because there is safety in numbers. Judging the safety and quality of an urban neighborhood is often indicated by the number of people who are out and about. As a pedestrian, it feels better to be surrounded by a few hundred others walking together, than to walk alone down a dark alley. If residents ever get bored, there's an active sidewalk just a few steps away to provide instant entertainment. The sidewalk can also offer a strong sense of community, or belonging, by the simple act of being around other people—even strangers.

Various groups often gather on active sidewalks to express their opinions. Preachers preaching their gospels, politicos addressing anyone within earshot, and protesters waving picket signs are commonplace on busy urban streets. When groups or individuals express themselves on a city street (no matter what the message), the surrounding area is quite apt to be a quality urban place to live. After all, few people picket the green of a suburban cul-de-sac. Urban neighborhoods with strong community spirit express it on their sidewalks and streets, and great city streets are bastions of free speech.

Local neighborhood streets and sidewalks are the urbanites' front yards. They are the best places to spend time and socialize. Neighbors meet on the sidewalks when they're doing such mundane tasks as retrieving their mail or walking to the bus stop.

Fun had by many at the City Market, Kansas City.

The Impromptu Walk to Wherever

The neighborhood sidewalks are even more packed than usual today. Something must be going on—what could it be? A large crowd is moving steadily to the east—where could it be headed? Quickening your pace, you join the determined march to wherever. How could this not have been on the calendar? Whatever this commotion is, something strange and big is happening.

The walk to wherever is becoming an enjoyable people-watching experience. One person trips on your foot, smiles, and says, "Sorry." Could this have been on purpose? You hope it is. After all, this person is kind of attractive. Others are involved in frivolous and loud conversations. Wherever everyone is going, the destination must not be a somber event. With all the laughter and smiling faces, wherever must be a fun place.

As the crowd begins to slow down, sidewalk space becomes scarce. This seems odd because there's no destination in view. As the crowd is growing, everyone gets quieter! And why are people painting each other's faces? Why are so many people gesturing? You finally realize that wherever is the annual City Street Mime Festival. Then a stranger volunteers to paint your face blue. You quickly decide to go with the flow. Who would ever have guessed that a new mime would be born today?

Urban streets are also functional. Local residents use them to search for food, run errands, meet friends, commute to work, take a jog, walk the dogs, pick up dry cleaning, or simply to disappear into the crowd. Most important, like most things urban, city streets are fun.

5. NOTICE CONSTRUCTION

Something exciting and contagious is happening in urban neighborhoods when many of their old buildings are being restored. Wooden shells are transformed into historic showplaces. Old warehouses become chic loft spaces. It only takes a few rehabilitation projects in an area to begin a full-on urban transformation.

Those old negative images of the city still exist. There are plenty of boarded-up crack houses, vacant properties, and razor-wire landscapes in American cities. What is changing quickly, especially in heartland cities everywhere, is how forgotten, almost empty neighborhoods are becoming highly attractive places again.

Urban places that are undergoing a metamorphosis are not always easy to spot. A sure way to identify them is by the presence of rickety metal support beams linked together vertically so rehab workers can do their jobs. In general, the amount of scaffolding visible is directly proportional to the level of interest and investment in a neighborhood.

Paying attention to where new houses, apartments, condominiums, and residential towers are being constructed is also important. These neighborhoods have the faith of developers who might otherwise be building more subdivisions in predictable, simple-to-develop cornfields and meadows. For developers, infill development (building on vacant properties, surface parking lots, or brownfields (tracts of land that have been developed for industrial purposes, polluted, and then abandoned) is very expensive and difficult. Local development processes often involve jumping through narrow bureaucratic hoops and untangling seemingly endless ribbons of red tape. Perhaps more than any other indicator,

New high-rise residential buildings on Cortez Hill, San Diego, are bringing hundreds of new city residents.

Scaffolding today means a beautifully restored home eventually in "Lafayette Square," St. Louis.

if new construction is surrounded by older structures, the neighborhood is an emerging high-quality place to live. Keep your eyes peeled for scaffolding and cranes.

The New Old City

There is a frenetic construction boom occurring on the east side of town, and you cannot help but notice it. Towering cranes are so numerous they almost rival the nearby city skyline. Concrete trucks come in and those hauling debris go out. New townhomes, condominiums, and single-family homes are being built on underused and ugly surface parking lots. Imagine—a new neighborhood built on a parking lot, forming where nothing but asphalt existed. Wow—a grocery store is on its way to serve residents, and so are a deli, restaurant, and nightclub. Signs that read, "Coming Soon—Luxury Condos," share space with affordable residential opportunities. This new neighborhood has its act together. You quietly say to yourself, "This will be my new home."

6. FIND PLACES THAT OFFER TRANSPORTATION CHOICES

Most city people own automobiles and use them frequently, especially if they have jobs in the suburbs. Cars are used extensively in most urban places, regardless of their population. The best urban environments, however, offer many other choices for getting around.

In your search for an urban lifestyle, find out how many transportation opportunities you'll have in a particular neighborhood. Is a reliable bus route nearby? Does the city have an aboveground train network or a subway, and, if so, where does it stop? How wide are the sidewalks, and how many people use them? Are there places to park a bicycle, moped, scooter, or motorcycle in front of local businesses? The more alternatives for getting around, the higher your quality of urban life will be.

Recently urbanized outlanders begin to appreciate these choices and to realize the freedom and convenience these options bring to their lives. Freeing minds and losing old-fashioned attitudes about noncar transportation are a result of life in a quality urban place. For instance, a city bus is no longer looked on as a slow ride, but as urban opulence: a chauffeur drives passengers to (or very close to) their destination while they read, talk, or enjoy the city scenery.

You'll find that city people have different attitudes toward transportation. They try to seek the "road less traveled" to find a stress-free and fun ride. For instance, while suburbanites get excited over a proposed freeway widening, urbanites try avoiding such roads altogether. Urbanites like commuter trains so they can avoid clogged highways and frustrating traffic jams. Using bike paths and bike lanes often can be faster than the freeway. Trolleys, ferries, monorails, electric buses— neighborhoods with these kinds of choices provide high-quality urban living. Having multiple transportation options (including the freeway) is perhaps the primary indicator of an authentic city lifestyle. Finding these places is very important.

The city is the place where people can be as expressive as possible in their transportation decisions. In the suburbs, many vehicles are used purely for recreation or hobbies. A pair of skates (or a scooter, moped, or a bicycle) can take people to actual destinations in the city. Seek out places where rollerblading to get breakfast, taking a train to school, or combining daily exercise with a power-walking commute to work are

A light-rail stop at Camden Yards, downtown Baltimore.

possible. Besides being functional, transportation freedom means having alternative and enjoyable ways to express individual personalities. It's a big reason why city living is attractive.

The most sophisticated cities are those that offer a range of transportation options. They accommodate people who choose not to own a car, or those who cannot afford one, without making them feel like second-class citizens. Even for car enthusiasts, cities with modern public transit systems generate a special kind of electricity that only comes from effortless transitions from one mode to another. The more transportation options available, the greater the degree of "big city" feel.

7. FIND GREAT URBAN PARKS

Although drawn to highly stimulating urban environments, city dwellers also need occasional relief from the crowds, noise, concrete, and hot

---

A Date and One Too Many

You are about to go on a first date. You catch a bus that drops you off at the train. The train is on time, and it stops just three blocks from your date's apartment. The two of you decide to go downtown to a movie, but the show starts in fifteen minutes. Luckily, the bus arrives just at that moment. The movie is great, as are the after-hour cocktails. You both have fun, but have a few too many drinks as well. No problem. It's late, and you both need to get back to your homes. You quickly hail two cabs, and, after a good night kiss, each of you is safely on your way home.

---

asphalt. Making sure that an urban neighborhood has at least one park is important. Parks offer much-needed spots for quick breaks or daylong retreats from the day-to-day stresses of the city.

The best parks have shade trees, elaborate landscaping, ample open space, cooling fountains, "pop" or classical public art, and interesting architectural features. Some offer summer grass for picnics and ponds for winter ice-skating. Others contain a good deal of formal hardscape materials (like concrete benches, asphalt paths, and stone monuments). Every day crowds of people wanting to escape from the rat race seek solitude, recreation, or a pleasant change of scenery and pace.

Urban parks can be as large as Manhattan's Central Park, where a variety of active (like frisbee-throwing or rugby) and passive (picnicking, reading, or napping) pursuits take place. They can also be as tiny as five hundred-square-foot pocket parks, which are great for people watching and conversing with new friends. Regardless of size, they contain features that tell weary city dwellers it is time to relax, rest, exercise, regroup, sort through problems, or daydream.

Urban parks feature inspiring city skyline backdrops, host festivals throughout the year, and offer enough foot traffic to sustain food and beverage vendors. Another exclusively urban park standby is the presence of pigeons scavenging for food as they waddle between pedestrians' legs. Perhaps the best measure of an urban park's popularity is the number of times dog "droppings" are picked up off its grounds.

Coolidge Park in Northshore, Chattanooga, has acres of open spaces, lush landscaping, a carousel, rocking chairs, rock climbing, and the longest pedestrian bridge in the world.

8. SEEK A WIDE DIVERSITY OF PEOPLE

The most inspirational urban places are those where residents enjoy living among and learning from different cultures and ideologies. Local cultural diversity is important because it usually means living in an open-minded neighborhood. The most exciting urban places are those that allow you to interact with people with different skin colors, ethnicities, sexual orientations, religions, incomes, and backgrounds. Although it may seem like negative reinforcement, more diversity means that it is less likely that you, whoever you are, will be discriminated against.

Socially diverse areas attract people from different backgrounds. Any combination of hippies, couples, freaks, singles, street people, gay people, geeks, artists, and corporate types are likely to become friends. A neighborhood might include skate punks, Christians, rollerbladers, drag

---

Urban Escapism

It is not even lunchtime, and today's work stress has raised your blood pressure to unhealthy levels. Paperwork is piling up, your voice mailbox is full, and the school called today because your kid is failing algebra. Finally— lunchtime is here.

The downtown sidewalks are too much to handle today. You need to avoid clients whose calls you haven't yet returned. And even though the city atmosphere is wonderful, the honking horns and chatter seem excessive today. The park is calling your name.

You find an entirely empty park bench right by the pond. A toddler and his father are fishing. The kid gets mad because someone's dog jumps into the pond and scares the fish. Everyone, including you, laughs. After all, the pond couldn't be more than three feet deep and surely doesn't have any fish.

The birds are swarming around bread crumbs. Lovers are starry-eyed on the bench across the way. The city skyline is shimmering in the sun. And your tension dissipates. The next five hours will be a cinch.

---

queens, atheists, rappers, Jews, fraternity boys, golfers, vegans, Muslims, students, bowlers, stockbrokers, cornbread eaters, sculptors, poets, shuffleboard players, singers, painters, sushi swallowers, martini sippers, and canned-beer drinkers. Laundry lists like this that describe people can be dangerous, of course, because someone or some group might be omitted! The universal rule of thumb when evaluating a high-quality urban area is to determine whether it has a wide variety of people and exhibits a wide array of interests and differences, rather than everyone being just like you.

Although suburbs are becoming more and more diverse, the difference in urban diversity is in the interactions that are forced by the city's close living quarters, sidewalk activity, and frequent cultural celebrations. Although urban neighborhoods are far from socially perfect worlds, insisting on diversity is a hallmark of city life.

9. FIND CREATIVE PLACES

Great cities encourage ideas to bounce off bricks and mortar and from mind to mind. Regardless of who you are, what you do, how much

---

Around the World at Work

You're a Caucasian from suburbia, but most of the people in your office are not. Your work team consists of people of Chinese, African, Korean, Mexican, Iranian, Indian, and Pakistani descent. More specifically, it includes a Chinese lesbian with a partner of twenty years, a black Southern Baptist minister who leads a five hundred-member congregation, an unmarried Korean bodybuilder, a Mexican national with a wife and family of five back in Monterey, an unmarried Iranian woman who runs marathons, an Indian man who recently graduated college in Great Britain, and a Pakistani woman who relocated last year from Sydney, Australia. The six-month project on which you all had been working has ended, and it was a big success. You consider the biggest success, however, to have been learning more about the people from all over the world without having to leave home. This is city life at its best.

---

money you make, or what you look like, as long as you're creative, you're home. Cities are home to what your suburban neighbors would describe as "weirdos." Living around a variety of "weirdos" should be a goal (*especially if you are a weirdo yourself*).

Richard Florida's book, *The Rise of the Creative Class*, described the emergence of a new demographic category that is growing by the millions. This segment of the population thinks for a living, values time as a precious resource, and innovates with high technology to establish wealth and influence. The book claims that geography is not dead. Even high-tech workers, who could connect their modems and computers to the outside world from places such as Jackson Hole, Wyoming, or even Antarctica, are choosing to live in communities around other creative people. Cities offer some the best places to do this.

Outside the realm of traditional business, city lovers need to know that they can be "weird." The best urban places encourage personal expression, whether it is manifested in something as simple as wearing fuzzy house slippers to the store, or as silly as dressing up like a bee and singing at the outdoor art fest. In the city, you can show off your tattoo one day and wear cuff links the next—because you can! None of these would be a big deal to anyone in a creative neighborhood. All kinds of experimentation and individuality (within the law) are welcome. The best neighborhoods allow people to break out of the suburban shell to enjoy a more open social norm that invites a wider range of expression and creative thought.

Creative urban places are as busy as they are fun. They allow residents to live around—even in—art. City areas that have a range of expressive opportunities for visual, performing, participatory, and spectator art forms are quality urban places. Neighborhoods featuring public sculptors, mural painters, actors, mimes, human statues, and lounge singers attract and cultivate more of the same. An urban neighborhood cannot have too much art or too many artists. The best urban neighborhoods inspire anyone and everyone to become artists themselves.

A spontaneous art infusion contributes to the overly used and loosely defined phenomenon known as "funk." A funky urban place is organic, raw, colorful, thought–provoking, and in your face. Funk is having the choice of a traditional play or an alternative movie. City neighborhoods should include plenty of funk and an abundance of creativity. (Funk is discussed further in chapter 6.) Few things are better for city people than living in a creative and funky community.

Transporting art in the Red Subway line stopping at Chelsea, Manhattan.

A Day in the Life of an Intensely Creative Community

The blues and greens swirl together in a manic pattern that is just right for the times. A bit of sienna and umber, and your still-wet masterpiece becomes worth viewing, maybe even worth selling. But there's no time to think about the opening at the gallery tomorrow. The group is coming over for a brainstorming session on your new idea—poetic software—where keyboard functions and the mind work together like poetry, offering a better way to work with data. Maybe there's enough time to get a fresh cup down the street, ahh, yes . . . just enough. Perhaps an electric outlet will be available for your laptop cord. Or, even better, someone, maybe even more than one guinea pig, will comment on the poetic software idea.

---

10. DETECT URBAN OPTIMISM

It's easy to detect a positive outlook in urban areas that are already active and alive. The optimistic faces of storekeepers, the pace of walkers, and the noise of construction tell of local success stories. Many urban neighborhoods are not as fortunate. They lack some or all of the previous nine items on the quality checklist, but they are still worth considering if they have something called *urban optimism*.

The American city has been under siege for decades, largely due to abandonment and economic disinvestment. Hundreds of urban neighborhoods have been ravaged by wrecking balls, crime, drugs, poverty, poor schools, weeds, litter, rodents, dilapidated buildings, and deteriorating infrastructure. Yet, many of these neighborhoods still hope for a better tomorrow. They should not be summarily discounted.

Inner-city neighborhoods that have strong and active community leaders and innovative business associations can be some of the most exciting and rewarding places to live: determined people who band together become hands-on urban activists with a common goal—improving local residents' lives. Such groups initiate planning processes to determine what kinds of land uses and architectural designs will best enhance their quality of life. They send representatives to development boards to voice concerns over objectionable construction proposals that might threaten progress (such as paving a parking lot or putting up buildings that look too suburban). They also celebrate every small victory—a new community center, a just-built playground, or a street landscaping improvement project. They toil diligently, lobby, and devote their lives to the big victory of the future—having their neighborhood become a quality urban place to live.

Try to see the great potential in a distressed neighborhood. A bit of research can disclose the residents' level of hope and activism. Analyzing what is occurring at street level usually is not enough. The local city government can provide more information, including contact names and numbers. Call these people. Ask leaders how you can become involved and whether you would be welcome. Neighborhoods with up-to-date Web sites also feature important news, current issues, and meeting dates that provide a revealing glimpse of the area's personality and level of optimism. Uncovering and joining an urban recovery movement can mean being a part of something exciting and meaningful.

Some places are more optimistic than others; some have issues that many people might not be willing or able to tackle. However, helping to turn blighted areas around can be a very rewarding—although difficult, expensive, and time-consuming—experience. Chances for real success and change in such urban places are often high as long as there is an apparent and determined optimistic spirit. Places that reflect this quality are tomorrow's urban showplaces.

Urban irony in Fort Worth, Texas.

The Signs of Optimism

Can anyone really live here? The buildings are completely abandoned, and the surface parking lots could cover the area of an entire small town. Trash blows down the streets like urban tumbleweed. But the colorful new banners tell the real story of what is going on here.

Banners bearing, "West Hill . . . Tomorrow's Urban Future," spelled out in crisp, white lettering on a bright red canvas background are placed on light poles everywhere—even in front of the unused parking lots and poorly maintained and abandoned structures.

After contacting the leader of the optimistic neighborhood group that started this place-marketing effort, you find out that she would appreciate your help. Like a religious calling, you feel compelled to make the banners' message come true. You have become an urban activist.

THE URBAN QUALITY CHECKLIST

Understanding the "Urban Quality Checklist" described in this chapter is the foundation on which the rest of this book builds. The following is a good example of a completed checklist. Learn how it works for your upcoming personal journey in search of your own center-city paradise.

SAMPLE URBAN QUALITY CHECKLIST

Date of Visit:

Urb Name: *The Short North* **(URB)**   *Columbus* **(CITY)**

Quick Directions: *High Street just north of the convention center*

Urb Type (circle one): Postindustrial   Garden   Eclectic

Blank Canvas

Neighborhood and Districts: *Arts District along the entire length of High Street, "Garden District" far north, Victorian and Italian villages are predominant neighborhoods (residential mix of housing).*

Check the following that apply:

1. Is it in a close-in urban location? Yes _X_ No __

How far is it from the downtown? _1_ blocks _0_ miles

2. Are there a variety of services and land uses? Yes _X_ No __

What kinds are most appealing or those that you would use regularly?

The art store, coffee shop, theaters, nightclubs, park with skyline views and a pond, grocery store, art galleries, record stores, clothing shops

3. Is there at least one mallternative? Yes _X_ No __

Where? What street(s)? *The entire length of High Street is a mallternative, easily walkable from all sections of the Short North. Big energy!*

What is there? *Coffee, art, fancy paper, candle, pet, and record shops; bars; ethnic restaurants; all kinds of great stuff!*

4. Are the streets and sidewalks active? Yes _X_ No __

How active? *Full sidewalks with many different types of people, street cafés, people walking dogs, waiting for buses, conversing, jogging.*

5. Can you tell if this urb (see chapter 3) **is growing or dying? Growing _X_ Dying __**

Evidence: *New apartments and lofts are being constructed on parking lots, scaffolding is found in front of many old historic homes, and people on the streets told me that the area has become a very attractive place to live.*

6. Does this Urb provide transportation choices? Yes _X_ No __

What kinds? *Excellent bus system, great pedestrian network, cabs, rollerbladers, scooters are all evident. No trains (unfortunately). Most residences have places to park individual cars.*

7. Does this Urb have a great urban park? Yes _X_ No __

What is its name? *Goodale Park*

Where is it? *One block west of High Street and south of Buttles Avenue*

How and when would you use it? *To walk my dog, enjoy the open space, to picnic, to watch and meet people*

8. Is a wide diversity of people evident here? Yes _X_ No ___

Explain: *I saw a mix of ages, races, people types, interests*

9. Does it seem like a creative place? Yes _X_ No ___

How do you know? *Huge art murals everywhere, like the* Mona Lisa, *art galleries, music clubs, and individual-looking people, "weird" and wonderful businesses.*

10. Does this Urb have "urban optimism?" Yes _X_ No ___

What did you detect? *Just talking to a few people at a coffee shop was enough to convince me that Short North residents love their area and are excited about its future. Absolute optimism. Fun place!*

BONUS SECTION:

Describe this Urb's energy and personality (including activity, vitality, events, moods, and rhythm [see chapter 3]**):**

To me, The Short North is "bouncy" and whimsical because all of the components of urban energy seem to bounce down High Street

Is this place congruent with your personality? Is this place *you*? Explain.

I'm weird, artsy, creative, active, expressive, and even "bouncy." The Short North matches "me."

Instructions for this crucial exercise, along with a blank checklist for you to take with you in your search, appear later in this book. Finding the geographic location of these places is also an essential element of your search; chapter 3 provides a "101" course to help you get there.

3

GETTING URBAN "101"

A ten-step minicourse that will help you find your authentic city life

Mastering the Urban Quality Checklist is an important start to finding a great city lifestyle. But, by itself, it's not enough. Suburbanites who graduate from the "101" course described in this chapter (combined with the principles in the Urban Quality Checklist) will be equipped with the tools they need to discover a great urban environment to call home. The tool kit includes ten important principles that readers must understand to acquire a basic education about the urban environment.

LESSON ONE: GO TOWARD "TRENDY"

A move to the city probably will be considered trendy, especially by suburban neighbors. Most people think of city life as trendy because the majority of Americans live in the suburbs. Today's American culture is suburban, and the majority culture is usually considered to be normal.

The lifestyle in the city is different because of its urban customs, architecture, transportation modes, and infrastructure, but, most of all, because of its urban setting. Cities are well established—even ancient. Trendy might not be the correct word to describe urban living. Perhaps it should be "retro?"

For instance, driving everywhere for everything and getting stuck in traffic for hours is normal, while taking a hundred-year-old subway is trendy. Because most people drive everywhere for everything, drive-through window coffee is normal. Walking to a sidewalk café and talking with neighbors while drinking that same cup of coffee is considered to be trendy. "Normal" means parking the car in a big surface parking lot before eating a fast-food burger, but it is trendy to enjoy a fresh hamburger in an outdoor market. Seeing a movie in a multiplex movie theater is normal, but choosing a seventy-five-year-old theater house featuring the same film is trendy. Working in a corporate campus in the suburbs is normal, but working in a restored office building is trendy. Living in a single-family housing development with a front yard and a garage is normal, but trendsetters live in converted loft apartment or condos downtown.

Examples of normal and trendy living could fill entire books. Just remember that trendy things are urban things; seek out trendy and discover urban life.

LESSON TWO: UNDERSTAND URBAN ENERGY

Most people understand the concept of urban energy because they have experienced it. It might have been in a city full of busy people, heavy traffic, canyons of tall buildings, thriving businesses, and music—a place where activity was buoyant. For those of us who love cities, these kinds of places are considered to be highly desirable because they are animated and full of excitement. They are so much fun that people consider them to be urban playgrounds. Visiting high-energy cities is a powerful experience because they exude urban energy.

In the process of choosing a city living environment (whether knowingly or not) people automatically gauge its urban energy level. Places with the "right" level of energy are places city people enjoy and want to live.

This lesson demonstrates how to develop an internal urban energy gauge. It also presents methods to better define and analyze what otherwise would be vague internal responses to this energy. A healthy combination of understanding urban energy and trusting gut feelings is important to making good decisions about where a new city home will be.

> ## Urban Energy:
>
> *The power generated and distributed by a city's activity, vitality, events, moods, and expressions that are sustained by the interrelationship among buildings, streets, and people.*

The study of energy is ordinarily a physics topic that involves a familiar formula: $E = mc^2$ (where energy equals mass times velocity squared). While this manual is far from a physics book, the idea of measuring speed and mass is appropriate to understanding how urban energy works. And while this book offers no hard and fast formulas, the general idea behind Einstein's well-known $E = mc^2$ equation can be applied to demonstrating how urban energy operates and how it can be detected.

Velocity is generated by human *activity* in a contained area—people in the act of "doing." Examples of activity are limitless, but might include walking, jogging, running, driving, eating, talking, buying, working, dancing, resting, celebrating, playing, browsing, and eating (among other things). Activity is the collective living of individual lives.

A city's level of activity is its *vitality*—the physical and intellectual vigor of the city's people. Cities with high levels of activity are vital places. Those with negligible levels of vitality are considered to be used up and unattractive. Still others, void of vitality, are "ghost towns."

Vitality can spawn city *events*, which produce city *moods*. Everyday events like the frenetic morning rush hour's traffic jams, honking horns, impatient (late) employees, and inevitable auto accidents produce various moods, ranging from apathy to exhilaration to stress. Lunch hour generates a more informal and relaxing mood. Jovial moods are triggered by holiday parades. Proud and celebratory moods come with cultural festivals, a local team's championship, or fireworks shows. Fun moods are caused by downtown concerts, food festivals, and carnivals. Protests cause angry and/or frustrated moods. Determined moods come from marches for a special cause such as curing a disease or promoting human rights. Worried moods grow from events such as a stock market crash or a country's declaration of war or news of an earthquake somewhere. City moods are *expressed* by collective faces of the city's people, many of whom are visibly active on the streets. It is possible to detect a city's expression on the faces in a crowd, its body language, walking speed, and collective human posture.

Five elements of urban energy form an integrated linear relationship. For instance, the city's *expression* changes with the general *mood*; moods change with specific *events*, which, in turn, affect the city's *vitality* and level of *activity*. This strong cause-and-effect relationship becomes the *rhythm* of the city. Urban rhythm is similar to an inaudible drumbeat governed by the tempo of the constantly changing elements of urban energy. The day-to-day pattern of a city's rhythm defines its composite *personality*. Each city's personality can be as varied as that of individual humans. For instance, they can be open-minded, easygoing, amenable, mean-spirited, compassionate, repulsive, fun, caustic, moody, industrious, lackadaisical, magnetic, flexible, dependable, or dramatic.

People choose friends based on their personalities and the contributions those personalities can bring to a relationship. Because a significant amount of time and emotional investment are required to build a friendship, choosing friends wisely is important. Personalities should complement, rather than clash with, each other. Likewise, the time, emotional, and especially financial investment expended in choosing a place to live—ensuring that a city's personality will complement, rather than clash with, your own personality—is crucial.

A city's true personality cannot be gleaned from travel guide summaries or based on hearsay. Beauty (and ugliness), after all, are in the eyes of the beholder. As though you are just meeting a potential friend, a city must be discovered, and time must be spent getting to know its inner workings and feelings, just as in considering establishing a long-term relationship. There are specific tactics for determining whether a city will be a suitable match. The best way is by understanding its energy.

Energy also can be generated in small towns and suburbs. It is the relationship that people have with the special city landscape (the mass of crowded streets and densely constructed buildings) that makes the energy "urban." Learning to identify and appreciate how urban energy works is essential, and, like other forms of energy, it must be generated, transmitted, harnessed, and distributed before consumers can use it. Because most people are familiar with electric energy, this form provides the best comparison.

Electricity can be generated by a variety of sources. Hydroelectric dams, car batteries, coal-burning plants, windmills, solar cells, or nuclear power plants are common energy suppliers. One or more of these sources must be tapped to provide a continuous flow of electricity. A combination of activity, vitality, events, moods, and expressions of the city's inhabitants generates urban energy.

Electricity is transmitted over power lines. These live metallic wires conduct power that is channeled efficiently from tower to tower. Urban energy is transmitted over city streets. Live asphalt corridors act as electric power lines, conducting energy and channeling it from block to block.

Electricity substations, dense collections of electrical conductors, harness electrical energy. They store the incoming raw electricity before it is distributed to households, offices, and businesses. Urban energy is harnessed by dense buildings constructed on city blocks. City buildings capture the incoming raw urban energy so it can be used locally by the people on the sidewalks, in cars, and in buildings.

Electrical energy customers are able to power their appliances, use their computers, and turn on the lights. Urban energy customers are able to power their spirit, feel excited about their living environment, and be inspired about where they chose to live. This is why exciting, vibrant cities are referred to as "electric" experiences.

Touching a live electrical wire, depending on the wire's voltage, will cause an electrical shock. Being in a city with high levels of urban energy (for someone who appreciates active, vital cities) will result in the individual being energized.

LESSON THREE: IDENTIFY URBAN STREET SHAPES

Because of unique biological makeup, every human being is different from every other human. Each of us has a specific DNA blueprint that determines every aspect of our development. Individual human cells combine to form organs such as hearts, livers, and lungs.

American cities are very similar. Streets create their "cells," which combine to make city blocks that form urban districts and neighborhoods. In the process of finding a city lifestyle and the right neighborhood, you must recognize the basic components of the city—its cells.

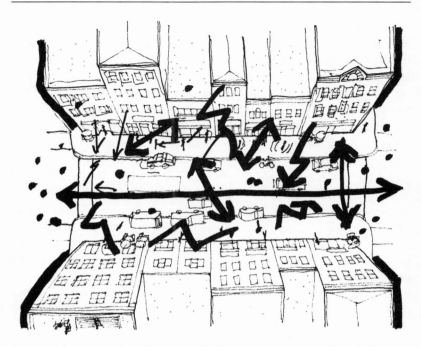

Arrows represent only a few of the thousands of movements and interactions of urban energy. It reflects from tightly packed buildings, down the street and into people. The interactions can range from slow and relaxed to frenzied. Pedestrians constantly come into contact with others. Noises dance in the air. Different smells fade in and fade out. All the senses are charged; even the city's taste is apparent.

Unlike the high-level complexities of cellular biology, finding the cells of a city is relatively easy; all it takes is a basic knowledge of geometry to recognize squares, rectangles, and triangles. Their cells have sharp, angular features and well-defined corners and points that can either be oriented right-side-up or on the diagonal—as long as they keep their rigid qualities.

There are exceptions to every rule, of course. Urban street shapes can be either perfectly or nearly round circles. Streets with circular or oval shapes are considered to be "urban" if they intersect with streets with straight lines. Truly urban circles should have at least three (preferably four or more) streets leading outward from them.

An urban "plan" is like a city's DNA, because it contains streets (like strands) that form a blueprint that guides how the city will grow and what form it will take. The plan also governs the shape of its streets and the patterns they will create in forming city blocks.

An urban grid is an ordered, rigid network of rectangles, squares, and triangles (and sometimes circles) that creates a web of angular city blocks. Pinpointing the street grid location in the city is vital because its interconnected blocks form a web that traps urban energy.

The design of an urban street grid encourages pedestrian activity, human interaction, sidewalk eating and conversing, and the expected commotion that contribute to the general city bustle. The pattern of urban shapes is predictable; they fit together like a child's jigsaw puzzle. Because the pattern encourages people to gather on the streets, the grid's simple configuration produces excitement and spontaneous behaviors.

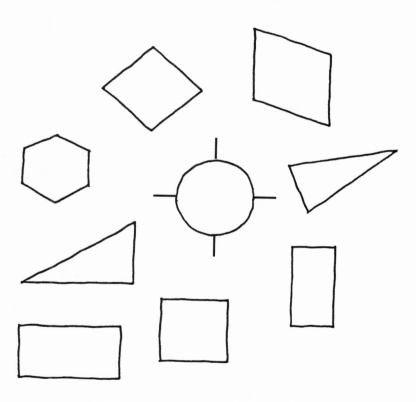

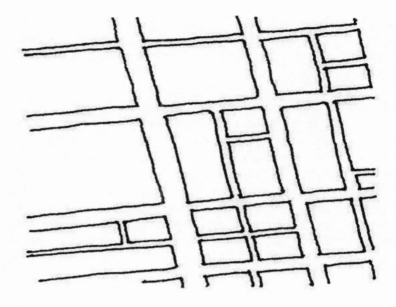

Grids encourage urban "districts," relatively small areas tied together by similar architecture or a specific function (such as Victorian architecture, theater, or meatpacking). Urban neighborhoods, also found on grids, contain larger areas than do districts and are usually associated with residential structures and local sustaining businesses.

The diagram on page 49 shows geometric shapes found in a typical city grid: rectangles, triangles, and circles. More complex, less perfect patterns are also common. The "DNA" of downtown Columbus, Ohio, in the illustration above, has squares and rectangles set at a slight diagonal but with no "squiggly" streets.

LESSON FOUR: AVOID STREETS WITH SUBURBAN SHAPES

Another important factor in the search for an urban environment is to identify *suburban* street shapes. The suburban version of DNA and its "cells" is vastly different from the urban kind. Instead of streets that form angular shapes and blocks, suburban streets form curvy, rounded, squiggly, and organic shapes. They resemble pollywogs, worms, pitchforks, eggs, crescents, fishhooks, cat eyes, balloons, and many other shapes. A good rule of thumb for identifying suburban street shapes is that if it looks like a cartoon character or something other than a primary shape, it's probably suburban.

There are exceptions. Streets that form squares or other angular shapes can be suburban if they are surrounded by suburban shapes. For instance, if a rectangle or a group of rectangles is alone in a sea of squiggles, the rectangles are suburban. Areas with angles surrounded by rounded shapes suggest that the location is far from the city's center.

Just as for cities, plans are the blueprint (the DNA) for suburbs as well. The suburban plan determines the shape the streets will take and the patterns they will develop. This usually means squiggly streets forming subdivisions instead of squares and city blocks.

Rounded and squiggly street shapes linked together are a phenomenon popularly known as suburban sprawl. The sprawl is formed by the various subdivisions and streets that have shapes resembling ears, lassos, hearts, and other forms that spread across the landscape. Understanding the location of the sprawl is vital, because it is designed to be void of urban energy. Suburban sprawl produces a vastly different kind of behavior from urban grids. It discourages pedestrian activity, human interaction, spontaneous sidewalk eating and conversing, and anything that suggests city bustle. The pattern of suburban shapes is illogical and somewhat mysterious. Although this configuration appears to be more varied and interesting than logical and ordinary squares and rectangles, city types find the lifestyle it encourages to be mundane.

Suburbs do not provide for districts or neighborhoods. Instead, they create subdivisions and shopping centers that resemble "pods." These pods almost always contain only a single land use (for example, a residential pod, a commercial pod, an office pod). Pods confine a specific activity in one location and are usually connected to each other by only one point. Each pod shape is usually independent of the others—kitty cats, amoebas, lollipops, and the like are all loosely linked together.

Pods are intentionally disconnected to produce "suburban" behavior—moving from one shape to another, usually by driving everywhere, parking in huge surface lots, shopping at suburban commercial strips, and an obsession with privacy that includes private drives, privacy fences, and private space inside cars. According to statistics, most people

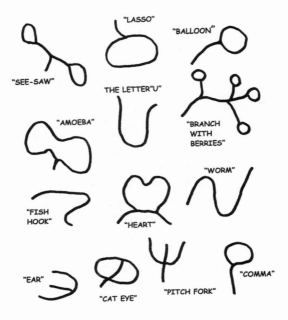

prefer this kind of lifestyle. People who want to become urban dwellers should avoid these weird shapes altogether.

The photograph on page 54 was taken from the air over a typical suburb. Suburban shapes are immediately recognizable, especially the long "worms" and commas. There are many more combinations of animated shapes found in this picture; try to find as many as you can. (Can you find the "kitty?")

Suburbs often have larger populations than do inner cities. Because people are the primary source of urban energy, this suggests that a good deal of human activity is occurring there. But suburban DNA encourages pedestrians to walk in meandering loops instead of on busy city streets, and it isolates workers located inside corporate campus pods instead of city blocks. In suburbs, eating is mostly done indoors or on a backyard patio, rather than at a sidewalk café or a park. The level of suburban activity often equals or even exceeds that of the center city, but the sprawling suburban street pattern hides any apparent vitality. In the suburbs, activity is hidden; in the city, vitality is readily apparent.

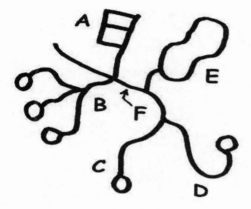

A. Angular shapes all alone surrounded by squiggles

B. A ladyfinger "pod"

C. A lollipop "pod"

D. A fishhook "pod"

E. An amoeba "pod"

F. The "worm" that links all pods together

Contained pods are designed to release energy immediately or to hide it completely. For instance, suburban events usually are much more subdued than those in the city simply because they are contained in pods that are isolated from everything else. Celebrations are confined to far-flung parks. Lunch is often at a drive-through restaurant. Carnivals are held in off-street strip mall parking lots. Concerts are often in open, grassy, out-of-the-way amphitheaters. Protests or marches do not work well in cul-de-sacs.

Because most suburbanites "hide" inside their homes or cars, few people are out of doors. This makes suburban moods hard to read or detect. The same thing is true for the collective suburban expression.

Some suburban shapes on this photograph include a snake, a comma, a woman's eye, a flattened corpse, a pitch fork, a kitty, a frowny mouth, a smudge, a jester, a worm, and a diary (among others).

Wide-open suburban strip malls with gigantic parking lots cannot produce, harness, or distribute urban energy.

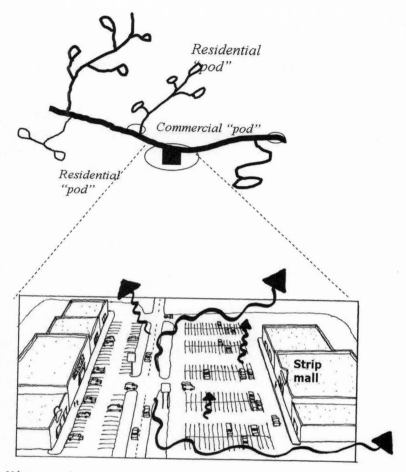

Urban energy that builds on suburban streets is doomed. Even if the street is straight instead of squiggly, energy escapes around the widely spaced buildings, around the cars, and through the trees.

All five elements of urban energy are muted in the majority of suburbs, so they all have very similar rhythms. And since suburban rhythm is oriented away from human detection or interaction, most suburbs are generally reclusive.

There is nothing inherently bad about suburban life. The majority of

Americans live in suburbs and love the lifestyle they provide. It matches their wants, needs, and ideologies. The suburban personality complements people who want to be alone, and most people do. However, this personality clashes with urbanites, who do not mind having their activity, vitality, events, moods, and expressions visible, exposed, and detectable.

Suburban energy is different from urban energy because of the relationships that people have with the suburban landscape (curvy streets, sparsely placed buildings), and it behaves differently as well. The use of electricity can demonstrate this reality more clearly.

Similar to streets in the city, suburban streets act as electric power lines, conducting energy and channeling it from pod to pod (instead of block to block). The differences end there, however.

Energy cannot be harnessed in the suburbs because of the lack of building density and the absence of rigid city blocks. Scattered buildings surrounded by parking lots and green space cannot capture incoming raw energy. The energy that exists in suburbs either disintegrates or evaporates.

Electrical energy customers can power their appliances, use their computers, and turn on their lights. Just like happy customers of urban energy, suburban customers are content with their lackluster, cloistered living environment and probably wouldn't choose any other. This is why the suburban experience is rarely described as "electric."

People who want to live in active, vital urban places are not likely to be stimulated in a suburban environment. In fact, you're reading this book because you want to find an "electric" urban lifestyle.

LESSON FIVE: RETHINK "CITY"

Just because someone says that he or she is moving to the city does not guarantee that person a city lifestyle. "City" is one of the most haphazardly used words in the English language. The concept of city is so evasive that even *Webster's Dictionary* offers only a vague definition. *Webster's* defines city as: "A place that is larger or more significant than a town." In most states any place, regardless of population or density, can call itself a city.

Three "cities" in Tennessee illustrate this dilemma. The City of Memphis has 650,000 people. The City of Lawrenceburg (actually a small town) has about fifteen thousand residents. A tiny village with around five hundred people calls itself "the City of Ethridge," demonstrating that even hamlets can be officially chartered "cities." Understanding that the word "city" is generally arbitrary, people in America seeking a city lifestyle must keep this in mind.

Avoiding confusion is especially important inside a city. The most common source of confusion is the excessive importance placed on artificially drawn municipal boundaries—the city limits. The common notion of living in the city or outside the city has become a function of whether someone lives on one side of the city limit sign or the other. Most cities outside of New York and San Francisco make it possible for residents to live in varying landscapes, including suburbs, the countryside, and even farms. The primary functions of the city limit boundary are taxing property owners and providing services such as police and fire protection. Many cities cover enormous areas, such as Columbus, Ohio, where it is possible to live nearly every kind of lifestyle, while still technically living in "the city."

The confusion does not end with the misuse of the word "city." Places designated as "towns" are just as varied and fuzzy. *Webster's Dictionary* defines town as "larger than a village and smaller than a city." This definition becomes meaningless, because it is difficult to find any towns and even villages smaller than "the City of Ethridge," Tennessee.

Suburban municipalities, regardless of how many people live in them, often identify themselves as towns or villages. The terms suggest prestige and seem to insist that these communities are not cities (with "cities'" obvious negative connotation). Some towns, like the "Town of Gilbert, Arizona," and the "Town of Cary, North Carolina," are about the size of better-known cities such as Albany, New York, and Hartford, Connecticut. Soon, these "towns" might be as large as Salt Lake City.

Suburbanites are quite aware of this phenomenon. A suburban village or town often has more severe traffic jams and smog than the nearby city's downtown.

Another distinction to be aware of is the confusion between living in the city and merely living within the physical boundaries of a metropolitan area. A good example is metropolitan Atlanta, Georgia, a huge twenty-county area measuring some 120 by 140 miles. More than four million people live in this region.

The city of Atlanta is merely a dot on a map of this huge metropolitan area that is as large as a small state. The only truly urban part of this region is so small that it is hardly detectable on the map. Still, people living in the remote hamlet of Jasper, sixty miles away, brag about living in "Atlanta."

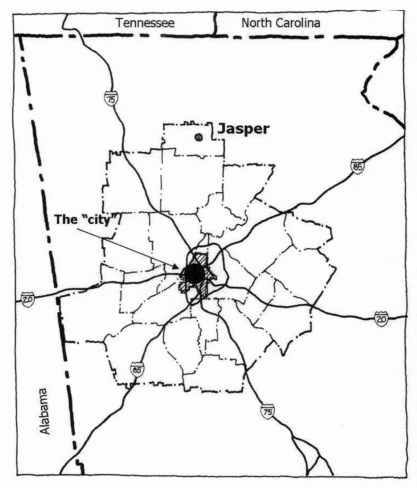

Most of this Atlanta metropolitan region has mountains, forests, farms, and especially suburbs. When looking for a city lifestyle, pinpoint target areas much more keenly than Jasper.

> ## Ignore the City Limit Sign
>
> *Place-names like "city" are vague and generally meaningless. When deciding to move to the city, you must decide what "city" means to you. If you just want to say that you live in the city, then none of these rules applies. If you are actually seeking an urban lifestyle, more research, awareness, and understanding are necessary.*

LESSON SIX: IDENTIFY THE AUTHENTIC CITY

This exercise calls for identifying urban and suburban areas in a practical way. Readers who have never been good at geography or reading maps shouldn't panic. The only skill you need is knowing the difference between a square and an amoeba.

Page 60 features a street map of the lower half of Manhattan. You can see that the entire map contains "urban shapes," mostly rectangles and squares. Two areas, Times Square and a section of the East Village, have been magnified to better show the street shapes. They are typical of the entire island of Manhattan, the surrounding boroughs of Brooklyn and Queens, and much of adjacent New Jersey.

Hundreds of rigid city blocks are apparent. The greater the number of city blocks linked together in this kind of urban street grid, the greater the amount of urban energy that can be harnessed and the bigger the city will look and feel. There are no curvy suburban shapes anywhere on this map. New York City has the most sophisticated, large-scale grid system in the nation. Naturally, it also looks and feels like America's biggest city.

Compare the New York map to that of Charleston, South Carolina (page 61). Two areas are highlighted on the Charleston map: "A," which is downtown Charleston, and "B," which is just across the water on James Island. These have been enlarged to compare each area's contrasting shapes more closely.

Area A, downtown Charleston, has urban shapes much like New York's. It features squares and rectangles (though not as geometrically perfect as those in Manhattan and with far fewer continuous blocks). Judging from the angular city shapes that form a clearly defined urban

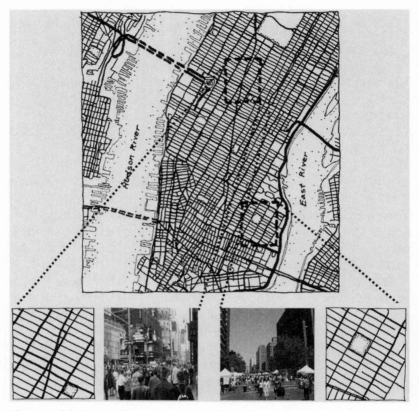

The unparalleled energy of Times Square. East Village's brand of urban energy.

grid, it can be assumed that downtown Charleston has a good deal of urban energy and is an authentic city.

The land in Area B is unquestionably suburban. Among the suburban shapes here are an "upside-down heart" and a "pollywog" (among others). Urbanites who want to live in the Charleston area should live on the "A" side of the water.

Identifying urban and suburban shapes on a map becomes critical when they are both within the "city limits." This phenomenon exists in almost every city in America.

Raleigh, North Carolina's urban shapes are found near the middle of

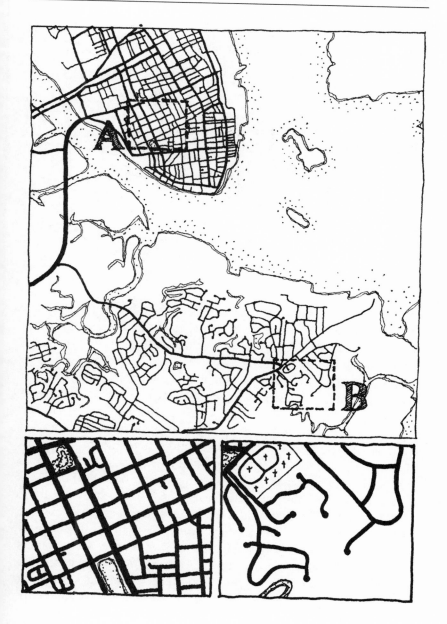

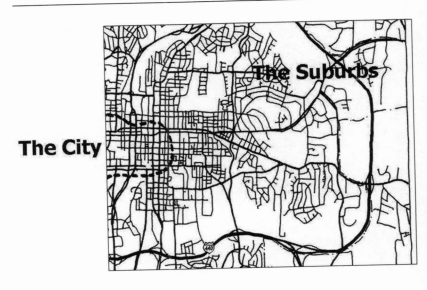

the city (above). Suburban shapes emerge quickly, far short of the outer freeway loop, and extend beyond the range of the diagram. Urbanites wanting to move to Raleigh have only a small section of city to consider when seeking an urban lifestyle.

It is often more difficult to differentiate urban from suburban areas in western states. The map (page 63) showing a section of Phoenix illustrates this difficulty. Most of the Phoenix area has angular shapes, suggesting that nearly all of the area shown on the map could provide an urban lifestyle. Western cities' street grid systems extend much farther outward than do those of eastern cities. Look closer. The grid is tightest and most compact in the lower right-hand side (east) in downtown Phoenix. The streets change shapes on the far left (west) of the map, creating "U" shapes and a few worms interspersed among the squares and rectangles. These are suburbs. The northeast (top right) is full of long rectangles, showing long streets with fewer access points than the shorter squares of downtown. This area probably will seem to be more urban than curvy, worm-shape streets are, but its location far from downtown suggests that this is an anomaly—a less curvy suburb. Watch out for this trick in western states. Urbanites moving to Phoenix should be sure to stay as close to downtown as possible.

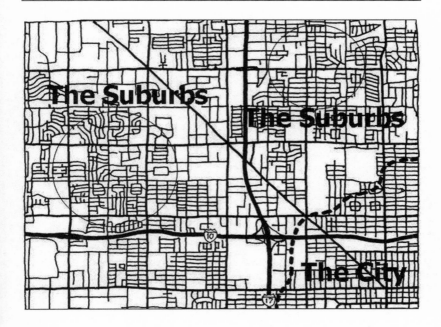

Another "trick" is found in cities with hills. The map on page 64 shows Chattanooga, Tennessee, a hilly, river city that has close-in neighborhoods that are actually very urban, but resemble a suburban pattern because of the uneven topography. North of the river is North Chattanooga, a decidedly urban neighborhood with streets that curve to allow navigation of steep hills. The area's close proximity to downtown is the first indicator that, without the hills, the city plan would probably have created a rigid grid if the land had cooperated. Although full of squiggles, North Chattanooga is urban because of its inner-city location.

LESSON SEVEN: CONCEPTUALIZE AN "URB"

As the root of the word, "urban," and the suffix of "suburb," Urbs are the target for people looking for quality urban living environments. Urb may be a strange-sounding word and not currently in many people's vocabularies, but it's the perfect word to describe a defined urban area

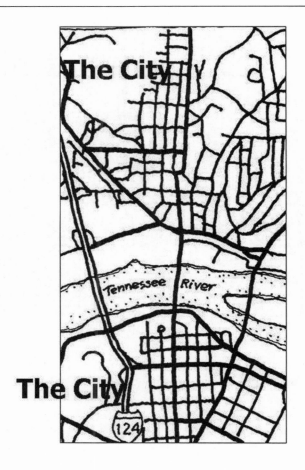

on a street grid where people live, work, play, shop, and thrive. Urbs have street grids and development patterns that harness and distribute urban energy. They are also the focus of the rest of this book.

Urbs are a configuration of urban street shapes and city blocks that combine to create districts and neighborhoods. Urb boundaries sometimes follow established neighborhood boundaries (as defined by the city or its residents). In other instances, especially when neighborhood boundaries split two sides of a street, an urb can contain several residential neighborhoods and multiuse districts (page 65).

Each urb is in a close-in location and should have active streets and sidewalks, rehabilitation and/or new construction, multiple modes of transportation, urban parks, diversity, creativity, at least one mallternative, and/or urban optimism. It should be possible to live your life inside an urb and never have to leave its boundaries.

Urbs offer human activity, various levels of vitality, and a range of events, moods, and expressions, all interacting with buildings, streets, and people. They are often the places that define the rest of the city and the region because they are interesting and exciting.

Urbs' residents support and keep current with local neighborhood development issues. Whether fully developed or just beginning to be redeveloped, urbs are typified by groups of people and individuals who want to see their area thrive. This nurturing attitude adds another special kind of urban energy that city lovers appreciate.

Urbs are sections of cities, like cities are sections of states. Thus, urbs are written by their name followed by a comma, then the city name, then the state, for example, *The Short North, Columbus, Ohio.*

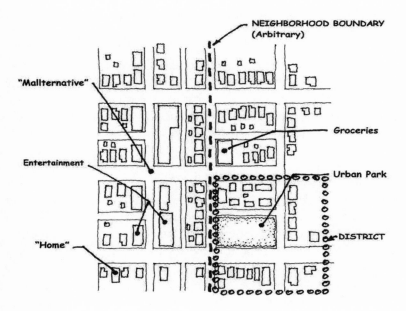

LESSON EIGHT: DETECT URB PERSONALITIES

Lesson Two demonstrated how to detect urban energy and the derivatives of that energy—one of which was an urb's personality. To refresh, an urb's personality is the composite of all of urban energy's components. Knowing and judging urb personalities can help you make a final judgment when you're choosing an amenable place to live in the city.

Just as no two snowflakes or fingerprints are exactly the same, so are no two urbs exact. Each has its own special look, function, and feel. Many even have their own smell(s). Understanding these subtle variations is important when choosing an urb to match your personality. Finding an urb personality match can increase your chances of being content in your adopted urban neighborhood.

Some people complain about the places where they live. (Suburbanites who read manuals to learn how to move to the city probably fit into this category.) Keep in mind that this phenomenon can happen in *any* upcoming move (even city ones) if the new neighborhood doesn't agree with who you are, what you stand for, what you'll see around you, and how you want to live. The urb's personality must be exposed to determine whether it's a good fit.

Most likely you'll "just know" that a place fits because it will feel like home immediately. While it's good to trust gut feelings, it's also wise to verify such feelings with other important signs. Looking more closely at an urb's personality will ensure that a place will be consistent with your wants, needs, personality, and financial investment. This process involves analyzing "themes" and "brands."

Detecting a Theme

All urbs have themes in various stages of development. The theme of New Orleans's French Quarter is "urban revelry" with a backdrop of Creole cuisine, Mardi Gras beads, spontaneous jazz, and Spanish architecture. Chicago's North Halstead has the theme of "gay culture," evidenced by rainbow edifices and gay nightclubs and restaurants. Downtown San Antonio's is "Venice Texas-style," with its canal, gondolas, and waterfront eateries. Downtown Nashville's Second Avenue's is "country music" and hosts huge two-step dance clubs, famous guitar shops, and western wear. Every urb's theme is mirrored on the landscape and marked by the local culture. You can interpret themes from the architecture, colors, activities, and customs that make places special. Some urb themes are phrases, like "Forever" (Buffalo's "The Elmwood Village") or "The New Urban Village" (Fort Worth South, Texas). To get a better idea of an urb's theme, try to find those that have written descriptions, so you're less likely to misinterpret them.

In addition to a short catch-phrase theme, some more progressive urbs publish descriptive literature, including short-story paragraphs that verbally paint a picture the locals want to convey. For instance, The Short North urb in Columbus, Ohio, further describes itself as a place of energy and excitement.

Cozy, quaint, sleepy little Short North—I don't think so

The Short North is anything but sleepy. It's full o' energy and excitement. It doesn't sleep. It naps—and not for long. But when it wakes up, it's with the smells of freshly brewed coffee and crisp newspapers. The whirl of bicycles. The clank of coins in an empty meter. The surprises. And the Short North is alive. Alive with people who love this area. And people who are discovering their own little secret for the first time. A secret of galleries full of color. Eateries serving up everything from eggs over easy, perfect bacon, and service a bit spicier than expected to the finest fusion cuisine this city has to offer. Shops crammed with hidden treasures. And nightclubs pounding with music. If you've never been to the Short North, get the hell out of the house. And if you haven't visited lately, don't you think it's long overdue? [excerpt from Short North Business Association literature]

Looking for the "Brand"

The most evolved urbs are like corporations selling unique products. They advertise their products using "brands," just like soft drinks, cosmetics, and cars. Looking at their logos, slogans, and images is an easy way to interpret the urb's theme further. If you like an urb, you can "buy" it simply by moving there and using the "product." More and more urbs are beginning to "brand" themselves for image recognition and marketing and to lure new people and businesses to their neigh-

"Sideways Mona" is the brand for the Short North, Columbus, Ohio. This brand does a great job of enhancing its energy-laden theme by suggesting "Art in your face!"

borhoods. An urb's brand is often featured on street banners, brochures, window stickers, even T-shirts and pins.

Some of the most energetic, interesting, and desirable urbs have defined their personalities clearly with their strong brands and descriptive themes. An urb is probably right for you if you get the urge to "buy into it."

LESSON NINE: BEWARE OF FAKE URBS

Fake urbs look and feel a lot like real ones and have very similar characteristics. They are often built on urban grids, have buildings close enough to the street to harness urban energy, and are usually packed with people most hours of the day. Their street scenes are active and can trick suburbanites looking for an active urban lifestyle.

Fake urbs sometimes have London-style phone booths on their sidewalks. Traffic cops often whistle cars to a stop for a crowd of people waiting to cross the street. They also can feature a network of spectacular fountains with dancing water. Park benches sometimes surround these fountains, where people sit and relax in the town square. Everything here is always strangely perfect. Trees along the street are all trimmed and exactly the same height. Street pavement is completely pothole-free, and sidewalks are clean enough to eat off of. Although fake urbs have no apparent "grit," they can be surprisingly authentic-looking city environments.

Fake urbs are often outdoor suburban megamalls with the usual conventional mall stores built on an urban grid. They can deceive many suburbanites into thinking they are real urban places. Look for such giveaways as directional signs in the parking garage that say, "Level Two: Town Center."

These "urbs" try to create the illusion of having neighborhoods and districts like real urbs. Some have named districts, such as the "Fashion District," and feature newly developed urban streets lined with mall stores. Some also feature residential "neighborhoods" offering apartments and condos to lure suburbanites looking for a city lifestyle. Beware—although these are often fabulous places, they are not the city.

These urbs seem fake because they are built on grids located far from the city center. Another reason they are not real is because they are usually surrounded by suburban street shapes. Looking at a street map or aerial photography reveals fake urbs that form "pods" linking only to other pods. Some have gates to keep traffic from flowing into a specific section. Curvy suburban streets take over immediately outside the urban-looking pod. A closer look reveals that the adjacent pods are subdivisions and strip malls.

Their fakeness becomes very clear when reading the "Code of Conduct" signs conspicuously placed in clear view along the sidewalks. Fake urbs are privately owned property with the legal right to enforce their own "laws," even to remove people from their land. For example, one fake urb conduct sign warns, "discourteous behavior" such as "standing, walking, or sitting that may cause an inconvenience to others will not be tolerated." Fake urbs are physically and ideologically far from the authentic city. Instead, look for connected places where freedom of expression within the law of the greater land is encouraged.

These developments are springing up all over the country. The malls on urban grids are sometimes called "lifestyle centers." Other residential pods disguised as urban islands are new types of subdivisions that use the adjectives, "neotraditional" or "new urban." Don't be lured by "neo" or "new" or "lifestyle" *anything* if you're looking for an urban environment *unless* they are built within and connected to actual close-in urban neighborhoods. Remember—new in the city should be surrounded by old.

In defense of the fake urbs, not all of them may be trying to fool suburbanites into thinking they are authentically urban places. Many claim that they "are what they are." Still, because most can easily pass the Urban Quality Checklist remarkably well, suburbanites can be misled easily by their "fluff and no stuff." Many are advertised as entertainment destinations that just happen to have living opportunities. Don't live there if you want a real urban lifestyle.

Just remember this simple rule, and fake urbs will never be a problem: Location, location, location always trumps lifestyle in your search for the city.

Be Alert and Beware of Fake Urbs

LESSON TEN: RECOGNIZE THE DIFFERENT TYPES OF URBS

Urbs have similar characteristics, but there are four distinct, easily recognizable urb types, all described in the next four chapters, to give you a better idea of which one might be the best fit for your next home. In summary, they are:

Postindustrial Urbs: Old warehouse districts, "used-up" historic industrial areas that have been transformed into quintessential urban living environments.

Garden Urbs: Quaint, tree-lined areas, often with historic or significant residential and commercial architecture. Garden Urbs are usually filled with single-family homes because they were the first suburbs on the extinct city trolley lines of the late 1800s and early 1900s.

Eclectic Urbs: These urbs have the most diverse mix of buildings, land uses, services and, often, "people types." In a "come one, come all" atmosphere, Eclectic Urbs usually have the highest levels of urban energy and are usually home to a good share of the city's funk (defined in chapter 5).

Blank Canvas Urbs: These urbs are relatively empty areas, often victims of the mid-1900s' urban renewal movement or struggling downtowns with too much empty space. Blank Canvas Urbs are for special suburbanites who have been "called" to be part of something. A full rebirth of these urbs is possible, and they have great potential for future vitality.

Note: City downtowns are always urbs, but can be any of these four types. For instance, Downtown Lexington, Kentucky, has a decidedly Garden Urb feel. Downtown San Diego and Cleveland are Postindustrial Urbs (although San Diego is building a new version). Uptown Charlotte is building an Eclectic Urb. Unfortunately, far too many cities—including Downtown Huntsville, Alabama, and Downtown Wichita, Kansas—are still blank canvases.

> *The following chapters feature the four kinds of urbs in more detail. They are differentiated to match individual tastes, wants, needs, and personalities with a proper urban environment. Each chapter also introduces urb examples from across America that fit into each category. Get to know them, so you'll be able to understand better how to find these kinds of wonderful urban places in the city of your choice.*

WHAT KIND OF URBANITE ARE YOU?

Determine which kind of urbanite you are by reviewing the four listed below. Because you can only live in one urban neighborhood, try to determine which one best fits your tastes, attitudes, and preferred living environment. Then go on to chapter 4.

Postindustrial Urbanites

- Find beauty in hard-core, edgy urban environments.
- Are drawn to strong, basic building materials such as steel, glass, and concrete.
- Think living in or as near as possible to the city's downtown is best.
- Consider "Up On the Roof" to be one of life's theme songs, not because of the music, but because of its message.
- Insist on stunning downtown skyline views.
- Don't consider groceries to be food unless they are bought in a public market.
- Are not pack rats and hate clutter—especially inside the house.
- Appreciate grass, flowers, and trees as pretty and nice, but not in front of the house.
- Love buildings with elevators, especially the old ones with steel lattice doors that require strong arms to open them.
- Like the privacy, security, and novelty of verbally screening everyone who comes to the door.
- Think that a little dirt and grit on the streets never hurt anybody.

- Consider modern interior designs to be most suitable to their tastes.

Garden Urbanites

- Enjoy small backyards where birds sing, fish swim, and butterflies dance.
- Think that digging in dirt is a human need, even when living in the city.
- Are perfectionists and would prefer their surroundings to match this aspect of their personalities.
- Regard front porches full of hanging baskets as highly desirable.
- Are often small-town folks at heart, but also like the idea of living in a city.
- Love traditional furniture, including classic or Victorian antiques.
- Have historic home revitalization on their list of "must do's."
- Think wood is good on houses, and old-fashioned red brick may be even better.
- Consider whitewashing a picket fence to be a good way to put the finishing touch on "home."
- Want fountains, especially ones surrounded by a big, formal park, as one the first sights outside their doors.
- Use the phrase, "Trees please," when consulting with their real estate agents.

Eclectic Urbanites:

- Are highly expressive, open to new ideas, and want to express theirs openly on the sidewalk.
- Are most apt to have adult deficit hyperactivity disorder and are easily bored, making it hard to stir their interest. They want to be stimulated as soon as they step out their front door.
- Get restless when their surroundings do not change frequently.
- Consider themselves, their friends, and their philosophies to be highly creative.
- Insist not only upon cultural and social diversity, but on architectural diversity as well.
- Are overtly boisterous and innovative and want the rest of their city neighborhood to appear this way.

- Sometimes consider themselves to be "freaks" and are proud of it.
- Are often total nonconformists.
- Have ideas of what "normal" means, and they are completely "abnormal" to most people.

Blank Canvas Urbanites:

- Consider the best things to be those that are "worth the wait."
- Are intrigued when analyzing "before and after" building photos.
- Do not consider an empty structure to be empty, just another possibility.
- Like to be challenged and are not afraid to tackle giant issues or problems.
- Do not mind living next to an empty building or a vacant property, if they know it won't stay that way forever.
- Consider themselves to be "influential" and want to practice working for significant causes.
- Enjoy establishing neighborhood groups from scratch.
- Appreciate the idea that they are affecting change in a positive way, and appreciate having their "thumbprint" on projects that are successful.
- Understand and accept the inconvenience of not having full-service grocery stores, entertainment, and shopping in the immediate vicinity, but are working on bringing them to the neighborhood.
- Like knowing they are the first people to live in buildings that have not been occupied in thirty years or more.
- Consider themselves to be hard-core "urban activists."

4

POSTINDUSTRIAL URBS

Every city has a "SoHo"

You Are a Postindustrial Urbanite If You . . .

- Like the thought of living in an avant-garde, edgy environment.
- Consider trees to be design accessories, not necessities.
- Like to buy food at open markets, farmers' markets, and other nontraditional places.
- Prefer balconies and rooftops to patios and backyards.
- Think "buzzing up" friends waiting outside is fun.
- Want to live as close to downtown as possible, and every linear foot counts.
- Appreciate pre–World War II industrial buildings, urban design, and modern interiors.
- Believe urban art is best inside a warehouse environment.
- Understand "just so" to mean as little furniture as possible.
- Desire substantial structures with concrete floors and ceilings, steel frames, and sturdy foundations.
- Enjoy having the best city views possible out of as many windows as possible.
- Get irritated when sidewalks and streets are "too swept."

THE RUST BELT IS COOL

Hugging the heavily industrialized Great Lakes region from roughly New York to Chicago is a region not-so-affectionately known as the "Rust Belt." Named because of the rust that was left over from highly concentrated abandoned factories and warehouses, the Rust Belt encompasses "worn-out" cities like Pittsburgh, Buffalo, Cleveland, Detroit, Toledo, and Milwaukee. Outside of New York and Chicago, the Rust Belt's image has been tarnished (literally) by urban blight and abandonment.

The Rust Belt has long been considered the last place anyone (even city lovers) would choose to live, especially when one could move instead to Sun Belt cities such as Atlanta, Dallas, or San Diego. But not anymore.

A Rust Belt environment is now hip, even in the Sun Belt. Urbanites are seeking Pittsburgh-like enclaves in Los Angeles, Phoenix, and Austin. Mini-Clevelands and Buffalos are emerging in Charlotte, Tampa, and Richmond. It is ironic that rust has become "cool." What is old has become new again.

Instead of places to avoid, "Postindustrial Urbs" represent the most authentic side of the city. Industrial urban edginess, associated with old factories and warehouses, provides the sharpest contrast to a suburban landscape and has become the "in" living space. "Edgy" and "real" are preferred by many over sterile, master-planned neighborhoods or contrived Disneyland-looking landscapes. Rust itself has become an attractive urban accessory to preserve and even showcase. It is ironic that the wasted places so many Americans have fled now represent the hippest, most quintessentially urban environments available.

SoHo STARTED IT ALL

The idea of living in rusty neighborhoods began in Manhattan's now infamous urb, SoHo. SoHo as an urb has become a prototype for American cities as a great opportunity to reuse and reinhabit throwaway areas of a city. It's the model urban neighborhood for dozens of heartland downtowns, including Birmingham, Knoxville, and Des Moines. The old, crusty building design is mimicked in "from scratch" city neighborhoods in East Village (San Diego), Copper Square (Phoenix), and the Arena District (Columbus). Whether it's an existing SoHo Rust Belt–like landscape or a completely new one, every city has a SoHo.

Before SoHo became *the* SoHo in the early 1900s, much of New York City's heaviest industry was located in lower Manhattan, just south of Houston Street (pronounced How ston) and bordered on the west by what is now Greenwich Village and on the east by Little Italy. By the mid-1900s, this area between midtown and downtown had become a highly visible zone of urban blight. Then the artists converged.

Although the area was known as "Hell's Hundred Acres," artists and other "weirdos" saw heaven. In the late 1960s and early 1970s, the old warehouses and factories became obsolete, and manufacturing abandoned the area. During this period, artists began crafting their work inside the shells of abandoned structures. The old factories' high ceilings, wide-open floor plans, stark plaster walls, and elongated, sun-filled windows were ideal interiors for creating. Setting the trends years before they happened, these artists were responsible for defining today's classic urban living. Contemporary urbanites of the twenty-first century now want the same raw features they had back then—exposed brick, plumbing, and support beams.

Artists became inspired by this special interior design and began flocking to SoHo, searching for available unused spaces. In just a few years, a large artists' colony was established, generating a hotbed of ideas and creative thought that were born in these old factories. There was, however, one glitch—this colony, according to the New York zoning code, was illegal.

Fortunately, the city ignored the law-breaking "squatters," but made sure that a sign that read "AIR" or "artist in residence" was posted at each building's entrance to let safety officials know that someone might be trapped in case the building caught on fire. Eventually, the zoning codes were changed to allow residential uses, buildings became safer, and SoHo was born.

After more than three decades as America's most revered artists' mecca, the resulting landscape has become classically urban. SoHo is now one of the world's food capitals, featuring five-star restaurants, outdoor cafés, and corner bistros. The French Culinary Arts Institute, which calls SoHo home, teems with chefs-in-training, all of whom are eager to prove themselves in local eateries.

SoHo boasts a multitude of art galleries featuring every available visual art. The area is now an international attraction for people who want to see a particular painting at the famed Guggenheim Museum, original sculpture at a local boutique, or home accessory at a number of shops. As a result, window displays engage pedestrians as they roam from gallery to gallery.

Like all of the best urbs, SoHo caters to people, not cars. Dense construction makes parking one's car difficult. As a result, pedestrians rule and bicycles are everywhere, used by seemingly everyone. SoHo's version of parking lots has become trees, iron works, light poles, and signs.

As refined as SoHo has become, there is still evidence of its grit. Graffiti is common, especially on the area's eastern fringes. The streets and sidewalks are still a bit dirty, and foul odors mingle with the smells of gourmet cooking. Even with decades of gentrification, SoHo has retained its gritty feel, which has been preserved as passionately as its old, historic industrial buildings.

Perhaps the most defining image of SoHo is its fire escapes. Locals adorn them with flowerpots and national and seasonal flags and use them to hang banners and signs advertising rooms for rent. Cast-iron balconies and staircases are more than lifesaving building code requirements; they are decorative and celebrated place-makers.

The power of SoHo's urban energy could not be contained within its urban canyons; it is a model of redevelopment that has spread slowly across America. SoHo-style arts and new resident artists have influenced urbs with similar industrial architecture. Forty years after the original SoHo was born, the idea of old/new industrial neighborhoods is fresh deep within the nation's heartland.

Nationwide, Postindustrial Urbs use the locational prefix, "So" (meaning south), and another street's first few letters to mimic the SoHo conjunction. For instance "SoLo" in Kansas City means South of the Lower Downtown Loop, where "Lo" is the freeway loop. "SoMa" is San Francisco's South of Market Street neighborhood. Others, like Denver's LoDo (Lower Downtown), want their urb name to rhyme with SoHo. Some urbs use "Ho" along with their entire cities, such as "ProHo," which means "SoHo in Providence," Rhode Island. These SoHo-like names bring an instant image, adding local novelty, New York urbanity, art-inspired innovation, and instant recognition.

The demand for a postindustrial urban lifestyle is growing in popularity. Established, emerging, and still waiting SoHos exist in every American city. This chapter focuses on the special elements that define Postindustrial Urbs such as SoHo. It also suggests a number of locations that provide excellent opportunities for living a postindustrial life outside of Manhattan.

THAT EDGY POSTINDUSTRIAL FEELING

Postindustrial Urbs share a common energy derived from a bygone era. Decades-old artifacts provide just the right kind of dusty, edgy, minimalist, hard-knock ambience. A few of the most typical postindustrial icons are shown on pages 80, 81, and 82.

SoHo is stark, bleak, and a little grimy—a perfect place to take your toddler for a stroll on a sunny day!

SoHo's famous wrought-iron fire escapes are visible on almost every building. These are SoHo's unofficial icons.

Clean and manicured streets are for indoor malls and subdivisions. Postindustrial Urbs are about imperfect gritty spaces like this hardscrabble café in the Arts District, Los Angeles.

Bolted rivets symbolize permanence, power, and strength—three features that make postindustrial places attractive to so many urbanites.

You are probably in a Postindustrial Urb when new loft spaces are advertised on hanging banners like this one. Postindustrial Urbs are often dark, stark urban canyons of old warehouses and factories.

The "buzz-me-up" box, a postindustrial icon allows visitors to press a button to announce their arrival. The loft resident is then able to confirm the presence of the expected party and "buzz" him or her into the building. These are found at common entrances, providing security and convenience for postindustrial residents.

POSTINDUSTRIAL MARKETS

Postindustrial Urbs are known for providing city residents with an unusual grocery-shopping experience. In a hardscrabble, old-world setting, food seekers are treated to an ambience that is vastly different from that of the typical, sterile suburban strip mall megastore. Whether indoors or open air, these markets are some of the most adored spaces in the entire city.

The primary difference is the special feeling evoked by urban markets' atmosphere. Industrial architecture, often historically significant buildings usually found in historic market sites, makes shopping interesting and enjoyable. Shopping trips here resemble those in Europe—people carrying single loaves of bread, a bottle of wine, and a recyclable knapsack chock-full of today's food. Customers exchange recipes with vendors and other patrons, and the market is often the community gathering place for the entire urb.

Like most things urban, a trip to the city market fuses art with groceries. Everything from innovative sculpture to crafts can be found here. Some have old-fashioned face-painting, ice-cream socials, and petting zoos for children. Others hold food festivals, book live acts to play music for shoppers, or hold seasonal celebrations. Markets also celebrate local traditions and customs. Needless to say, markets are also great places for people watching, experiencing new ideas, and meeting eclectic new friends.

Shopping at postindustrial markets is never the same experience twice, but it is a novelty every time. A variety of fresh food is the reason. This novel ambience often lures the best restaurants and well-known chefs who choose to live within walking distance of freshly cut meat and recently harvested produce. Organic and ethnic food enthusiasts often find the best selections here as well.

As festive as the urban ambience can be in these markets, food is always in the spotlight. "Foodies" converge on the markets to hover over the products from local residences and throughout the greater city area. Postindustrial markets are destinations because they encourage people to spend a lot of time thumping melons, squeezing ripe fruits and vegetables, smelling the aromatic flowers, and exploring new vendors' goods. It is easy to understand why, considering their ambience, they have become postindustrial place-making icons.

The Loft—Quintessential Urban Living

Unpartitioned residential units inside old factories and warehouses, known as "lofts," are usually distinguishable by their concrete floors,

The North Market in Downtown Columbus, Ohio, is the grocery store for the "urban carless" and a playground for outlanders.

towering, multipaned windows, exposed bricks and mortar, uncovered plumbing, and suspended air ducts. Loft interiors have open, airy designs with clean lines, sharp edges, steel beams, and ornamental rivets. They are the predominant postindustrial home.

Lofts can have elevated bedrooms dangling from reinforced steel cords or perched on support structures over the open living space below. They also feature a predominantly open living space with fifteen- to thirty-foot-high soaring ceilings. Many of these buildings were constructed before World War II and often were designed (or strongly influenced) by only a few development companies. As a result, most architectural specifications are universal—whether in Des Moines, Boise, Winston-Salem, or SoHo.

Of all loft elements, their undefined spaces are what make them special. Unlike the traditional house with permanent walls and fixed rooms, lofts provide a multiuse, open layout that is perfect for painting, sculpting, and other artistic trades. Their uncluttered design can accommodate computer work spaces, photography studios, or hobbies such as yoga or cooking in an expansive gourmet kitchen. The loft interior blends every aspect of life into one big room.

Loft living is the new way to be old-fashioned. Just as cobblers and bakers of yesteryear lived above their workplaces, lofts provide a modern version of this old way of life. Being located in one of the most mixed-use parts of the city, loft residents can work just below their place of residence in a shop or sidewalk business or set up a workshop in their own home. Such arrangements provide a much-coveted staircase commute, thereby eliminating the need to join daily traffic jams and stressed-out rush hours. Many people without creative hobbies or small studio businesses are attracted to lofts as well because they are considered to be the ideal personal urban residence. The ideal loft experience usually places residents very close to the center of city action, bustle, amenities, and excitement. Residents are an elevator ride or staircase away from morning coffee and sidewalk cafés. Nighttime entertainment (microbrewery pubs, nightclubs, great restaurants, and a host of other amenities) has long been associated with Postindustrial Urbs. Loft residents can take advantage of their close proximity to a wide array of enjoyable activities to do after dark.

Lofts usually are associated with bold colors highlighting unique industrial interior features, experimental and expressive modern art, plate glass showers, and tall walls that paint pictures of shadow and sun. Some residents use portable sections or temporary partitions to create the room-of-the-day or to establish privacy in a favorite corner.

Today, especially in cities where old warehouses are becoming scarce (like New York and Denver), where few existed (Houston), or where those that did have been torn down (as in Charlotte and San Diego), "faux" lofts are being built with features similar to those found in rehabilitated historic structures. These structures may or may not have a hanging bedroom, but they are always open and airy.

Sturdy and substantial old industrial buildings can now provide quality city living opportunities in the Historic Third Ward, Milwaukee, Wisconsin.

Imagine functional fun always waiting just beneath your window. Lofts in Postindustrial Urbs provide easy trips to everyday activities (SoHo).

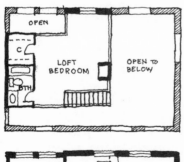

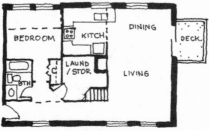

POSTINDUSTRIAL STYLE

Crisp clean lines, bold colors with cool undertones, and modern decor are characteristic of postindustrial interior spaces. Lofts' open floor plans and high ceilings usually are embellished with steel furniture, lacquered wood, and sleek fabrics. Oversize art, especially tall canvases that almost touch the ceiling, provides symmetry and balances the room. Lighting and other accessories often resemble what might have been used in the factories that lofts replaced. The postindustrial interior is the opposite of "country"-style décor—this is not Grandma's house.

As the most urban of interior designs, postindustrial style often is associated with minimalist art. Abstract, geometric, fluid, and clean minimalist interiors are intentionally uncluttered living spaces. As simple as it sounds, this is arguably the most challenging look to achieve.

Occupying large, open spaces with minimal furniture and other accessories has come to define chic urban living. Having only a few pieces of furniture renders each chair, table, and painting a singularly bold statement. The pieces become art themselves; they stand alone waiting for guests' critiques and inevitable comments. Residents often give careful thought to the placement of sofas, tables, lamps, and even towels, just as they would in creating an object of art. The intensity and perfection that minimal interior design requires in the wide-open environment of the postindustrial residence go far in exposing the occupant-designer's personality.

Minimal postindustrial style has many important benefits: residents do not need to purchase much furniture; everything that is displayed probably will be "liked" if items are displayed so indiscreetly. And, best of all, if something does not fit or gets tired, removing and/or replacing that singular object can have a dramatic effect.

Are You a "Postindustrialist?"

The rest of this chapter explores postindustrial urban America. Each urb described resembles the look and lifestyle of SoHo, but is special in its own way. By understanding the personalities and opportunities of these national examples, you will be able to find your own Postindustrial Urb in any city.

THE OLD MARKET, OMAHA— "SO OLD"

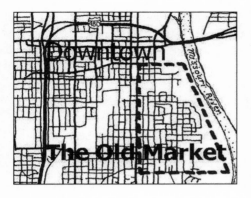

Once it is fully introduced to the nation, Omaha's "The Old Market" will become an icon of urban America. City seekers will be intrigued by this eclectic Postindustrial Urb despite its ho-hum Nebraska address.

Like SoHo, this is a high-order arts enclave that insists on creative expression. The built environment is filled with innovators living in old historic structures on cobblestone streets and shadowy alleys. Its SoHo-like design inspires painters, writers, musicians, and actors.

Cutting-edge alternative theaters offer high-shock-value plays and introspective one-person shows. Small venues feature stand-up comedy, poetry readings, and modern tragedies. Even the Old Market's sidewalks aren't strangers to impromptu street performers. Locals also appreciate classic plays that offer an alternative to the ubiquitous left-of-center performances. "Way off Broadway" can be interpreted as a compliment here.

Strolling the streets becomes a personal interpretation of the visual arts. Open-door galleries invite pedestrians inside to view paintings, photography, and sculpture while New Age or techno music sets the mood for a featured artist. Art galleries are scattered everywhere—tucked inside back doors, on main corridors, downstairs and upstairs. The arts scene is so pervasive that Old Marketeers wouldn't be fazed in SoHo.

The center of The Old Market is a hodgepodge of all kinds of services. Most of them have to do with art, but there are also many urban novelty-based restaurants and a variety of events that drove the district's economy years ago. Beverly Hills–style services thrive here as well—Swedish massage and meditation therapy spas, yoga schools, opera houses, Euro-flower shops, and a diverse selection of fusion bistros, including those featuring Mediterranean-Italian and Arabic-French cuisine. You can still order the city's most freshly chopped steak or down authentic Irish ale.

Sophisticated urbanites appreciate the functionality of an urban convenience store with exposed brick walls, live plants, and retro-tiled, black-and-white, checkerboard flooring. Old elevator doors open, emptying residents onto the sidewalk. Locally grown fresh produce and exotic items from countries throughout the world can be found just a few short steps away at the market. The variety of food alone makes living here an enjoyable experience.

Luxurious and eclectic services are appreciated, but they are not what make The Old Market special. This urb becomes too good to be true in that it is a wonderful, high-quality, full-service urban neighborhood in a kind of old-world "Oz." City types love it here because of the Manhattan-style arts, but they stay because of the down-to-earth services and Midwestern sensibility.

Neighborhood issues are common to most other Midwestern urban neighborhoods, including noise during the wee hours, crime watches, and controversial development proposals. The Old Market also hosts a

The Old Market is ahead of most urbs in attracting a full line of services and an increasing number of permanent residents. Above-storefront lofts such as the one seen here are popping up along many streets.

"Dickens Christmas" celebration (as would be expected in the heartland) where people exceed their already over-the-top friendly threshold. This is very much a heartland urb, but with a Manhattan twist—"pigeon control" is at least as important as traffic control.

A touch of Manhattan can be found in The Old Market, especially in the Jones Street Corridor, restored warehouses that probably were considered expendable just a few years ago. Jones Street is fast emerging as one of the most cutting-edge urban living experiences west of the original SoHo. Surprisingly reasonable rents attract a brilliant mix of older couples, young singles, and middle-aged people set on an urban pilgrimage.

In full SoHo-style, paper coffee cups warm palms as early risers stroll back to their renovated lofts after preworkday conversation. Others schlep bags overflowing with fresh vegetables. Businesspeople walk home from downtown Omaha office towers carrying bundles of dry cleaning over their shoulders. Dog walkers wave to joggers who smile at the occasional person dripping Missouri River water. Kids holding ice-cream cones whiz by on neon-colored skateboards, young adults don rollerblades, empty nesters stroll down the sidewalks, and sweat turns to steam during the dance club crowd's stumble back home. Enthused urbanites are sure to find this urb to be their idea of urban heaven.

SOUTHSIDE, CHATTANOOGA— "EcoSoHo"

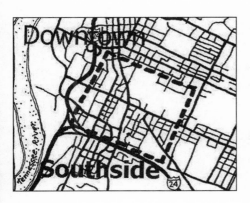

To appreciate Southside Chattanooga, fully requires a trip back in time, to about twenty-five years ago. Approximately one hundred acres of heavily concentrated, particularly noxious factories belched smoke or sat lifeless, burned out, and unproductive. Southside was an ugly place and one to avoid if you could. Avoiding Southside was difficult, however, be-cause it was adjacent to downtown Chattanooga.

During the 1970s when most of the factories' black soot was par-ticularly obtrusive, the intelligent way to pass through was by driving a car—fast. On approach, one took a deep breath and made sure all air vents were closed. Sometimes, headlights were needed at noon because black and gray particles turned day into night. Soot covered outdoor workers' clothing and hair. Visible air pollution often be-came trapped in Chattanooga's deep Appalachian valley walls, which contributed to the coining of the city's regional title, "Armpit of the South."

What a difference two decades can make! From the poster child of environmental degradation and home to major U.S. Environmental Pro-tection Agency superfund sites, Southside Chattanooga has reversed its role. The turnaround had much to do with its dramatic cleanup and newly earned title: "The Environmentally Sustainable Urb."

Still a work in progress, Southside acts like a former chain-smoker turned health nut. Since the late 1980s, most of the factories abated their smelly nuisances or closed down. Local industries stopped their air pol-lution to such a degree that Chattanooga's air became the cleanest of any city its size. Southside then began to build infill developments that, with the help of the city's splendid natural features, began to resemble the principles of feng shui (the balance of nature and design).

For instance, Southside is blessed on four sides with "wooded" mountain vistas (Lookout Mountain to the south, Missionary Ridge to the east, and Raccoon and Signal mountains bound the western and northern views). Rusty industrial factory shells were transformed into shiny public pavilions representing "metal." Red and brown brick buildings represent "earth." Flashing neon lights from the famous Chattanooga Choo Choo Hotel sign, jazz clubs, the brightly lit, in-your-face college football scoreboard, and the glow of the downtown skyline at sunset provide "fire." Ancient side streets have exposed "stone" pavers. "Water" exists not only in scenic outdoor fountains, but also flowing freely in the Tennessee River that bends sharply just over the horizon.

Eco-oriented projects are conspicuous everywhere, all winking and nodding to the industrial past and contributing to a sustainable future.

The new Southside elementary school opened in 2002. Built specifically for downtown employees, its superior building, high technology, and excellent teachers provide a catalyst for an emerging Southside residential boom.

The new University of Tennessee football stadium was constructed among the intricately preserved smokestacks and factory shells. A "green parking orchard," where parked cars are cooled by green leaves and grassy storm water intakes, welcome fans. Rainfall is captured and pumped into curious-looking, thirty-foot-tall phalluses. There are also plans to implement an eco-industrial park where one factory's waste is the adjacent factory's raw material. Any conservationist would love it here.

One of the Southside's most amazing features is that real families with real kids are beginning to move here. Although there are few grassy backyards (and no cul-de-sacs), Southside is home to a brand-new downtown neighborhood elementary school. The school building's handsome architecture resembles the surrounding factory shells and is providing a stimulus for building a city neighborhood that is demographically similar to that of a typical suburb. It also puts Southside into a category by itself—traditional Postindustrial Urb singles, childless young couples, empty nesters (and other "weirdos") who appreciate the happy, unusual urban sounds of playground noise and a landscape of jungle gyms. Southside is a growing family-oriented place in the most unlikely surroundings—smooth angles, metal borders, textured glass, modern art, and "soccer moms."

THE HISTORIC THIRD WARD, MILWAUKEE—*"SoHIP, SoNICE"*

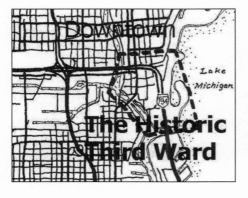

No one would have believed only two decades ago that being the buckle of the Rust Belt would be so good for a city's future. Milwaukee, long known for beer brewing and heavy industry, has had (and for some, still does have) a negative image as being dirty and used up. For anyone who has ever harbored negative images of Milwaukee, a trip to The Historic Third Ward will be a jolting experience.

Smashing all Rust Belt and old Milwaukee stereotypes, this area seems more appropriate for champagne than beer. Bowling is still popular, but so is sculpting. Youthful energy, regardless of an individual's age, has infused sophistication and pride into the area. Creative types have fortified the neighborhood with art, entertainment, and beauty.

Like many Postindustrial Urbs, The Historic Third Ward is a celebration of life through art, and art is everywhere. There are enough venues to support "Gallery Nights," inviting both locals and suburbanites to fill studios, restaurants, and middle-of-the-street pocket parks. Enthused art lovers converse, critiquing traditional oils, modern acrylics, and contemporary black-and-white photography, and put on formal attire to attend the theaters. Opera is hip, as locals attend exuberant performances for a dose of drama. The Historic Third Ward is for "presenting yourself": doing it up and having a blast seeing and being seen.

The Historic Third Ward has a large mass of creative capital. Dance companies call it home, and advertising agencies and high-tech firms draw interns from the Milwaukee Institute of Art and Design's campus and dormitory. There are a lot of forward thinkers here, and innovative newcomers can expect to find a home sweet home. The setting is awe-inspiring, but it could not have been possible without having once been a hard-knock industrial neighborhood. It survived a devastating

The Third Ward adver-
tises itself as Milwaukee's
Arts District.

fire in the late 1800s that destroyed many square blocks; then it suffered the devastation of fifty years of urban flight to the suburbs.

Today, the creative arts and entertainment sectors have come to the
area's rescue. In spite of its hard-knock history, The Historic Third
Ward thrives and is one of the best examples of how to maintain a community by changing and growing despite potentially devastating circumstances.

The Third Ward boasts old five- to ten-story warehouses that are
new again, a shiny architectural wonderland that has polished away
any unwanted rust (but kept the rest). The structural intrigue is height-
ened by residents, who obviously cannot get enough of their prized
balconies. This is most apparent along Water Street, where loft livers
use them to shake out dusty rugs. Neighbors talk with one another by

stretching their heads over, up, and down as they hold on to wrought-iron rails. Breakfast on the balcony becomes a boat-watching show as vessels coast down the Milwaukee River below, slowly making their way to nearby Lake Michigan.

Balcony bums succumb to street-level temptations like "Festa Italiana," a huge celebration of all things Italian, and Summerfest, a musical event that draws thousands. The Riverwalk, a smartly designed pedestrian trail, also encourages people to enjoy the urban environment.

Perhaps the best aspect of life here is the blending of authentic big-city living with over-the-top friendliness. Patrons, joggers, bicycle cops, and sidewalk strollers seem compelled to say "good morning" and "how are you," wave, smile, and make eye contact far more than expected. Imagine . . . an ultrahip but down-to-earth Postindustrial Urb with extremely nice people!

RIVER MARKET, KANSAS CITY— *"SoHoMO"*

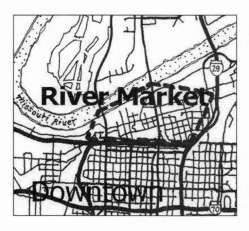

The River Market District has long been Kansas City's best place to find delicious pastries, gourds in season, the hamburger of your choice, fine spices, used clothes, and even a live chicken. The atmosphere is the opposite of a suburban mall and is much grittier than the popular Country Club Plaza historic shopping destination a few miles south.

Especially on Saturdays and Sundays, the River Market is vibrant, exhilarating, and fun. It's a people watchers' destination that provides a photo opportunity on every corner. Spectacular skyline views and city grit make River Market a novel, authentic destination.

Local boosters of the River Market District advertise their area just north and down the hill from downtown Kansas City as the place to get an "urban fix." Suburbanites have taken the bait and flock here, especially on weekends. After twenty years of being a getaway for outlanders, something more exciting than a weekend day trip is occurring here.

River Market is becoming a magnet for full-time residents. Several affordable and upscale historic loft rehabilitation projects have been completed on SoHo-like Delaware Street. Throughout the urb, surface parking lots and vacant properties are becoming endangered species. New mid-rise apartments and condominiums provide full-time life and energy, turning the urb into what it's supposed to be—a neighborhood.

Locals can walk out of their five-story buildings onto a pedestrian walkway that links to the fresh market. Those who work downtown have an easy commute—less than a ten-minute walk. Hard-core urban Kansas Citians can now live in a vital postindustrial atmosphere every day, not just during Saturday business hours. Country Club Plaza, eat your heart out!

The celebratory atmosphere of the River Market.

Shockoe Bottom, Richmond— "Soto(bacco)"

Shockoe Bottom, Richmond's old tobacco mercantile district, dates back to the seventeenth century, one reason for its prime location along one of the East Coast's premier pedestrian riverwalks. It is also adjacent to Richmond's most fashionable shopping district, Shockoe Slip, which is host to one of the oldest farmers' markets in America. The historical charm of Cary Street and bustling, dense Downtown Richmond are located close by.

One of Shockoe Bottom's future loft buildings receiving much needed attention. Popular activities in this urb include tearing, sweeping, abating, vacuuming, hauling, and repairing—preparing for a population and vitality explosion.

The Bottom has fewer great urban destinations than the more-established surrounding urban enclaves. This will not be true for long, however; this area is undergoing an astonishing redevelopment/ rehabilitation building frenzy. Its burgeoning success and popularity are assured because of its proximity to the nearby urbs and because of its impressive stock of fashionably ancient warehouse buildings.

For an urban enthusiast, Shockoe Bottom is exhilarating because of its incredible focus on reconstruction. If a warehouse has not already been gutted and restored to better than its original splendor, it is in progress. Windows are huge, trim is ornate, and urbanites who like quality living are ready to move in.

Street-level and rooftop spaces are already attracting restaurants, re-tailers, and other businesses that are quickly turning Shockoe Bottom into a model mixed-use urb, even in its as-yet-unfinished state. A critical mass of residents has settled here, and their demand for services is spawning grocery stores, dry cleaners, and neighborhood bars. It's already home to many great restaurants.

At its present pace, Shockoe Bottom could soon become America's most beautiful, interesting, and livable Postindustrial Urb. If you have doubts about what an old city can do to transform itself, a trip to Richmond is recommended.

BRICKTOWN, OKLAHOMA CITY—"SOBRICK"

Bricktown is the best urban enclave in Oklahoma. In fact, it is well on its way to becoming the best such residential area in the Southern Plains region. Its theme, "as much red brick as possible," gives it a consistency and character all its own. As Oklahoma's only thriving SoHo, Bricktown "wows." This is more than "okay" city living, and it's getting even better.

Bricktown consists of many rehabilitated warehouses, several restaurants, offices, a festive canal, and a lot of red brick. The streets are paved with red brick, the buildings have brick facades, the new baseball stadium is brick—almost everything is brick, brick, BRICK. This otherwise ordinary building material defines the urb. It is impossible to mistake where you are—Bricktown.

Its locally famous gateway, an old railroad overpass (one of the area's few nonbrick edifices), welcomes visitors to the brick bottoms. As a result, increasing numbers of suburbanites are choosing to play, shop, and live here.

A new urban-infill town house development has been completed on Bricktown's north end, just up the hill from Sheridan Avenue, the main drag. This is a great start, but Bricktown needs thousands more residents. There is still room to build: a few surface parking lots and vast, vacant prairie land on the east side are likely to bring more full-time residents and more everyday services. Bricktown's potential is too great for this not to happen.

New restaurants and apartments are bringing new life to Bricktown.

Although it borders on being too perfect, Bricktown's Riverwalk is as urban as it gets. Not unlike San Antonio's Riverwalk, the surrounding businesses, urban design, and public art provide a merry atmosphere and a pedestrian's dream. There are water taxis full of people (especially during baseball game days) that shuttle drivers from their cars to the stadium and transport others on leisure rides.

Bricktown is considered a retail, lodging, sports, and entertainment district today. Soon it will be considered an excellent residential choice for urban Oklahomans and city lovers everywhere. "City" is finally a legitimate adjunct for "Oklahoma."

DOWNTOWN MEMPHIS— "SO-SOUTHERN"

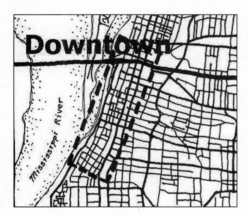

The word, "Memphis," conjures up images of Elvis, hot Mississippi Delta nights, and a slow-as-syrup lifestyle. What many people (perhaps even the locals) don't know is that for city types, *the* urban "good life" is Memphis. The entire urb is southern SoHo, featuring the best of old and new grit.

Development crews crank out structural magic on surface parking lots and the few vacant corners left. Magnificently designed condominiums and rehabilitated above-storefront lofts have added to the 25,000 people already living in the downtown core—more than all of the urban core residents of the combined downtown populations of a dozen southern cities.

Downtown Memphis is so great that it's hard to pinpoint its best urban experience. World-renowned Beale Street would be the obvious choice. With so many new locals, this is becoming a neighborhood haunt as well as a national tourist attraction. Beale mixes the sound of horns and aromas of dry ribs fixed "Memphis style." North of Beale, a

Most of downtown Memphis, including this trolley, retains an Old World ambience.

frenetic new loft construction is occurring around the new minor league baseball park. Few cities make it possible to watch a live baseball game, eat a steak, and enjoy cocktails all on a private residential balcony.

Although most Tennesseans would never admit it, the center of downtown is a lot like gritty New York. Its old-fashioned mid-rise structures and urban canyons would make Manhattan residents feel right at home. Yet, downtown Memphis distinguishes itself with an old-fashioned, bell-ringing trolley instead of a subway and ribs instead of crème brûlée. "Y'all" and "urban" blend in Memphis.

DOWNTOWN DAYTON—"*CHIC-HO*"

Not many people would guess that Downtown Dayton, Ohio, is architecturally intricate and stunningly beautiful. This relatively unknown area in southwestern Ohio is transforming from scruffy to chic. High-energy, creative people are arriving with moving vans for a piece of the fabulous urban environment. Something big is happening here.

The metamorphosis was spawned by a renewed interest in the many beautiful industrial structures in the heart of Downtown. Absent the smoke, soot, and foul odors associated with heavy industry in the early to mid-1900s, these numerous three- to ten-story buildings are some of the most substantially built and striking postindustrial edifices in the world. Just as striking is the renewed interest in returning here—Downtown Dayton was left for dead several decades ago.

Today it's suddenly fashionable. Hard-core urban locals appreciate the urb's combination of SoHo and European influences. It is "European" because of its street system, reminiscent of broad Parisian boulevards featuring cutting-edge public art. Intricate monuments, statues, and overhead electric bus lines add to the urban ambience. Graceful, wide sidewalks comfortably accommodate pedestrians with enough room for sidewalk cafés.

Most of the new residential activity is occurring along St. Clair Avenue and points east. "The Fire Block," a designated historic district, is a model for new rehabilitation in the remaining magnificent, but still boarded-up, structures. Many building rehabilitation projects here are inspiring.

Locals who have not been to Downtown in years will be amazed at what was hidden beneath ugly aluminum siding. Removing the vast facades displayed grand doorways and huge windows awing metro Day-

This recent renovation, "The St. Clair Lofts," has received national attention, proving there was an urban residential market and sparking a full-on return to Downtown movement.

ton city lovers—and will inspire national postindustrialists looking for a home.

Structures come alive as orange sunlight reflects off the tall metal beams and glass. Hard-core yesteryear reveals itself in imprinted masonry and majestic rotundas. Dark, romantic shadows that are cast inside deep concrete valleys mix noon with midnight. Colorful awnings mark finished rehab projects, and scaffolding announces residential opportunities coming soon. This landscape is gritty-glamorous, visual, and visceral.

In addition to its superior loft structures, the urb has a superb public market, several art galleries, ambient outdoor cafés and coffee shops, and nightclubs for every scene. The lifestyle offered here is best described as big city in a small package. The arts thrive as well; Downtown hosts the philharmonic orchestra, opera, ballet, and several theater companies. Already a lot like a little New York, this urb is becoming increasingly jam-packed with activity. It's going to get even better—revitalization is just beginning here. When complete, Downtown Dayton could become one of America's chicest Postindustrial Urbs. Life here, even in the often-bypassed city of Dayton, Ohio, will be hard for any urbanite to resist.

THE STRIP, PITTSBURGH— "PITTHO"

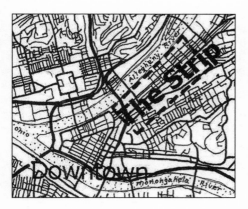

There is a very narrow urban area just east of downtown Pittsburgh that locals love and newcomers are discovering. "The Strip District" is a linear mile of hundred-year-old buildings occupied by unique businesses, trendy restaurants and bars, and ultraurban residences.

The Strip is a feeling—refreshingly old and soiled. It is the opposite of a "master planned" district. The architecture, which doesn't seem to have changed since before World War II, will return you to the days of Shirley Temple, the Little Rascals, and the Three Stooges.

Even suburbanites wonder what it would be like to live here. Walking to work in nearby downtown, enjoying the riverfront, and frequenting the historic market all beckon, and redevelopment is beginning in earnest. Lofts are

being built in old warehouses and provided as new buildings on former parking lots. The Strip is defining a new Pittsburgh image—old *and* cool.

HISTORIC CORE, LOS ANGELES— *"MANHATTAN, CALIFORNIA"*

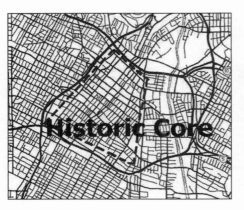

Los Angeles has long been known as the "freeway capital" and the epitome of suburban sprawl. Its most famous icons, including Hollywood and Venice Beach, are both miles from downtown. Rodeo Drive, the region's most revered fashion district, is in another municipality—Beverly Hills. Many Americans have no idea that Los Angeles is America's most industrial city. Even more don't realize that it has a high-energy SoHo clone in what Los Angeles' downtown locals call the "Historic Core."

The Historic Core shocks unsuspecting visitors expecting a sprawling "Los Angeles." Its eerie resemblance to Lower Manhattan, particularly Broadway where it approaches SoHo, provides exactly the same Manhattan-style energy. The Core is packed with pedestrians, street vendors, schleppers, and shoppers. The diverse population reflects many colors, ethnicities, and audible languages mixing in the urban canyons (mostly Chinese, Japanese, Spanish, and English—a lot like Manhattan).

It's hard to imagine that residential opportunities have begun emerging here recently because the area appears to be as lived-in as New York. The Historic Core has just begun to repopulate the upper floors of several warehouses and toy factories. Many office buildings have been converted into residential loft spaces, as evidenced by huge banners advertising "Trendy Lofts" dangling out their windows.

"Start spreading the news!" Los Angeles' Historic Core is an excellent big-city experience.

New residential construction is announced by architectural renderings on "coming soon" billboards. At street level, the Historic Core has more apparent residential advertising than does any other district highlighted in this book.

The Historic Core's success is assured because it is the only such landscape in Southern California. Popular residential outlands like Orange County, the beaches, the Valley, or the "Inland Empire" cannot offer this kind of exclusively urban environment—just like Manhattan. It is a novelty, unknown even to the locals who never had a reason to come here. Now they have a reason to live here.

WASHHO, ST. LOUIS— "MANHATTAN, MISSOURI"

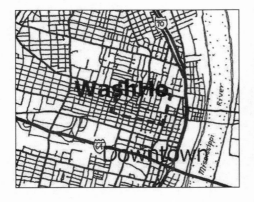

WashHo (named by the author) combines SoHo and St. Louis's Washington Avenue Loft District. Washington Avenue is the Midwest's best answer to Manhattan. Unlike booming downtown Los Angeles, WashHo has yet to take off. It's not yet full of pulsating energy and vibrant street life—but it will be soon. WashHo is currently undergoing a total rehabilitation.

This is St. Louis's best postindustrial offering. All the elements are here—a tight grid, lots of mid-rise buildings, and a big Manhattan-style

In a New York state of mind—the extra-urban, gritty, and wonderful Washington Avenue corridor.

feeling. But St. Louis has been one of America's most serious victims of severe urban disinvestment, not unlike Detroit. WashHo's local model is quickly helping to turn the city's famously negative image around. It provides St. Louis with a beautiful, ultrahistoric, increasingly high-energy urban experience. City lovers will be encouraged to see so many recently abandoned, outdated, and crumbling ten-story garment warehouses turned into stunning, rehabilitated "high-style" residences for those who want a St. Louis city life. It's about time.

OLD TOWN, WICHITA—"THE NEW OLD WEST"

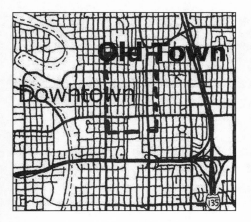

Old Town, Wichita, has a heartland personality with a laid-back, Kansas-style ambience as refreshing as it is calming. Though lacking the cutting-edge Old Market, Omaha flair, or the chic style of downtown Dayton, it fills an urban niche—down-to-earth city living. This could be the most "balanced" Postindustrial Urb.

Spaghetti and meatballs or sirloin steak are as easy to find as sushi and caffe lattes. Depending on the mood, dessert could be bananas Foster as easily as a banana split. A haircut could mean going to a Euro-style salon this weekend and an old-fashioned barbershop the next. Nighttime establishments see early baby boomer crowds giving way to teenagers on first dates, followed by "geared-up" weekend revelers. Choose a black Irish stout tonight and a sparking red Cosmopolitan martini tomorrow. Old Town accommodates everyone, regardless of taste, income, or mood.

Like so many Postindustrial Urbs, this one is named for a historic farmers' market. The market's two faces perfectly define the greater area's personality. For instance, bins are divided between farm-fresh, just-picked Kansas vegetables and chi chi sun-dried herbs. Arts-and-

Old Town is cozy and old-fashioned but with a Manhattan-style flair.

crafts vendors chat with abstract oil painters with foreign accents. Old-fashioned, handwoven baskets blend with exposed brick. A banjo or a harp could be serenading outdoor shoppers. The venue's proper name, the "Wichita Farm and Art Market," couldn't be more perfect.

Land uses are pleasantly balanced: Old Town lures art galleries, eclectic dining establishments, communications firms, and comedy clubs. Historic hotels-turned-luxury-apartments and simple lofts whose residents live and work in them share similar addresses. Rehabbed buildings with high-tech start-ups neighbor old factories. Amateur poets and professional columnists work here. Old Town suffers gladly from an unusual form of split personality disorder.

The past and future also balance perfectly. Cobblestone streets, historic arch entryways, and ancient Old West brick structures blend with forward-looking (but historically appropriate) new office and retail construction. "Freaks" donning headphones and kneepads gleefully skateboard alongside farmers and cowmen. Few urbs blend past and future, young and old, West and East as delightfully.

Until now, few urbanites would consider moving to "rural, insignificant Wichita." As one of America's best Postindustrial Urbs, locals must be prepared to house thousands of people, especially well-rounded postindustrialists who cannot help but want to move here. New housing opportunities are emerging, and, fortunately, many vacant and underused properties north of Old Town proper may be available for an impending city-lover onslaught. Look for the full-time residential supply to increase with an already high demand.

FINDING THE POSTINDUSTRIAL URB(S) IN *YOUR* CITY

Other than attending a public marketplace or restaurant, suburbanites often do not "see" urbs, especially if they are just beginning to emerge. For urbanites, Postindustrial Urbs are easy to find, and every city has one. Those unsure about where to begin to look in their city can use this simple method to find a new SoHo-style neighborhood.

First, pay attention to the side of downtown with old warehouses, factories, and abandoned factory shells. Then find one or more of the following within close proximity to the old industrial structures:

- A low-lying area around the downtown. Industrial areas usually were in floodplains or near rivers. If a city has an area using the word, "bottoms," in its name, it is likely the Postindustrial Urb.
- Railroad tracks. Heavy industrial factories of the past relied on the railroad to haul raw and finished goods to and from their destinations. For factories and warehouses of the past, railroad tracks were the equivalent of today's freeways. Postindustrial Urbs almost always have one or more sets of railroad tracks.
- A city market. Fresh produce arrived on the railroad cars in the old days. Markets were functional long before they were chic, and many have survived as important historic landmarks.
- For sale or for rent banners. If you see a big cloth banner hanging from a warehouse or old factory building, you have found the Postindustrial Urb.
- Brewpubs. Microbreweries flocked to Postindustrial Urbs during the 1980s and '90s. Places to drink a freshly brewed beer downtown are often located in a Postindustrial Urb.

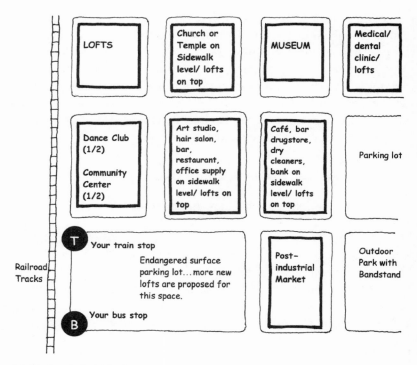

Model of postindustrial urb.

- More "stylish" graffiti. Of all urb types, artlike graffiti is most likely to be found in the alleys of Postindustrial Urbs.
- Any reference to "SoHo" in a business or residential building name.

> *You should have enough information now to find a Postindustrial Urb in any city you choose. Does a Postindustrial Urb sound like it's for you? Before you answer, consider the next chapter, which describes "Garden Urbs," a completely different urban environment.*

5

GARDEN URBS

Every city has a Savannah

You Are a Garden Urbanite If You . . .

- Fantasize about birdbaths, fishponds, and outdoor thermometers as much as you do the city itself.
- Like to tackle a major historic home rehabilitation.
- Seek plank siding over steel plating and certainly over vinyl.
- Get excited when you see picket fences.
- Insist on a patch of ground, no matter how small, and will not compromise.
- Think that lots of trees are important in an urban environment.
- Prefer everything in your neighborhood to be more "perfect" than the typical urban neighborhood.
- Consider a neighborhood with too many mixed uses (for example, industrial and manufacturing uses) to be too much as a place to live.
- Are drawn to traditional furniture, architecture, and interior design.
- Want to have front porches and potted plants on staircases.
- See yourself as a small-town person who just so happens to want to live in a city.

- Gravitate toward grassy, formal, open parks with ponds and fountains.

It's Cute. It's Quaint. It's an Urban Garden.

While most city neighborhoods are defined by the local architecture, Garden Urbs are neighborhoods where vegetation takes the spotlight. Homes are in harmony with nature, buildings are garlanded with flowers, and streets are dignified with uniformly spaced planters. Because the environment is elegant and stately, the pace is slower than that of the surrounding city full of concrete and asphalt.

These substantial, quaint urban neighborhoods are deep inside the city, but were once on its fringe—the first suburbs. They were often places where wealthy bankers, lawyers, doctors, and other prominent residents built their grand houses near the country while having the convenience of trolley lines running into the central city. These first

Embellishment of any feature (windows in this case) with plants is typical of Garden Urbs.

These neighborhoods are likely the most overtly patriotic of all urbs. The architecture and pre-dominance of front porches just call for flags.

suburbs were just far enough away from the soot and filth of the old in-dustrial city, had the most beautiful streets and the best schools, and were considered to be a great place to raise families. Now these former suburban communities are decidedly urban and are some of the most endearing city neighborhoods.

That feeling of wealth still remains. Urbs in this category were built to last because rich people had the money to build the biggest houses with the most expensive, highest-quality building materials. The work-ing class also lived here, too, in smaller but just as significant family homes. Regardless of house size, construction crews were not allowed to skimp.

Garden Urbs are also manicured. Original residents insisted that the streets and sidewalks in front of their homes be adorned with decora-tions as ornate and lush as those in their personal gardens. With such attention to detail, it's no wonder they are some of the most beautiful sections of cities.

Picket fences are a top icon in Garden Urbs.

After World War II, most influential people (even their neighbors and employees) began moving to the next layer of suburbs (the ones we're more accustomed to), leaving most of these original neighborhoods in disrepair. Because the average person couldn't afford to maintain mansions, they transitioned into multiunit apartment buildings. Others were abandoned altogether. All too often, beautiful, historic homes were demolished to build freeways to accommodate the growing number of suburban commuters. Those homes that remained intact have become some of the hottest real estate for today's urbanites.

Because of the demolition and neglect during the urban flight of the second half of the 1900s, a good number of Garden Urbs established new protections for their neighborhoods, the most effective of them being the historic zoning district. These districts require both new construction and structural rehabilitation to mimic the period in which the older structures were built. Specific types of building materials that predominated in their original construction have become mandatory,

The ground in Garden Urbs is mostly brick pavers, often accented with wrought iron or green ivy.

for instance, using historic brick instead of vinyl siding or maintaining original wood that has been scraped and painted—not replaced. These districts have banned demolition as well, saving untold numbers of historic structures. The effect has been tremendous. Most of these neighborhoods have new luster, resembling their glory days.

Garden Urbs are normally the places suburbanites seeking to return to the city feel most comfortable moving. Perhaps it's because these neighborhoods were indeed suburbs at one time. Their high-maintenance homes are filled with weekend warriors fighting against time—sawing baseboards, repairing and replacing plaster walls, sanding and sealing original hardwood flooring, and planting bulbs in front lawns. Garden neighborhoods have become tourist attractions because they stand out gloriously, softly, and elegantly from the rest of the edgier surrounding city.

Regardless of geographic location, the feeling is ubiquitous.

Whether in New Orleans, Kansas, Arizona, or Connecticut, all have the same qualities—they are quaint "small towns" within cities. It's not surprising that they are usually home to most bed-and-breakfasts in the city.

THE PARKS OF GARDEN URBS

Garden Urbs are greater parklands. Their sidewalks are adorned with shady trees, hedgerows, decorative streetlights, brick pavers, and park benches. Street corridors act as linear urban pathways, attracting pedestrians, neighbors, and runners to enjoy the scenery. Cars often drive more slowly through Garden Urbs because of the inviting, calming effect of the surrounding historic architecture and intricate landscaping. These are not places drivers want to rush through—there's too much beauty!

Formal parks here are often the most elaborate in the city. Grand monuments and sculptures of historic figures are placed in conspicu-

ous locations. Mature trees often have expansive canopies, and flowers are in abundance. Walking trails, either paved with brick or padded with crushed stone or mulch, attract birdwatchers, butterfly catchers, and bulb planters. Some parks have lavish ponds that become skating rinks in the winter, and those that are stocked with fish draw children equipped with poles and bait in warmer weather.

Anytime during daylight hours, dog enthusiasts socialize alongside their canine counterparts. Kites fly on windy days. Skaters take advantage of sunny days. Impromptu croquet, horseshoe-throwing, or bocce ball matches during the afternoon are cleared away for jazz or classical concerts held in the gazebo in the late evening.

It's easy to see why park enthusiasts are drawn to these neighborhoods. Having urban park access with pulsating city life just a short walk away is the ultimate in luxury.

LUSH GARDENS

Garden Urb residents love their neighborhood parks so much that they try to bring a little bit back home to their yards. Typical lots here are long and narrow, with homes that are only a few feet from the sidewalk. This kind of front-heavy layout creates a quaint urban street scene, and, at the same time, it provides an abundance of outdoor living space in the rear yard. This private park space is then forced to lie between the back door and the detached garage on the alley.

Decorating these skinny backyards is an obsession for many homeowners as they prepare for the local neighborhood home and garden tour (a long-standing tradition in Garden Urbs). Observing from a second-story rear window, residents usually see a succession of elongated parks. Neighbors peek over to see what new inspirations their friends have implemented. A goldfish pond, a minigreenhouse, or a new piece of lawn sculpture are common projects.

Backyard urban gardens have become signature expressions of a typical Garden Urb resident and serve as an oasis for less hard-core (as compared to Postindustrial) city types. Because their backyards are often tiny, every square inch is used. Gardens often feature a birdbath, planter, stone, flowering annuals intricately placed among low-lying

ground cover, and an informal, mulch-paved sitting area. Other gardens are more formal, with brick instead of stone forming more defined edges, and old-fashioned, wrought-iron fence creations.

Urban gardens provide ready-made hobbies for flower and landscaping enthusiasts. Residents also use them for functional reasons, like outdoor gatherings and Sunday teas. More than anything, they are for the personal enjoyment of the people who created them (as well for showing off).

Urban gardens are so important to many urbanites that such people would only consider a city lifestyle if they were assured an opportunity to undertake their own garden masterpiece. Garden Urbs attract urbanites who literally need to dig in dirt and to be surrounded by nature—but within a city.

Old Homes

Besides the gardens, another perk of Garden Urbs is the abundance of historic homes of all shapes and sizes. Whether a huge restored man-

sion or a character-injected shotgun house, a home is inappropriate for many urbanites unless it's old, and most older and intact residences are in garden neighborhoods. These homes come with the previous residents' life stories. They typically have qualities demonstrated in the above photograph.

THE MODEL GARDEN CITY—SAVANNAH

Of all American cities, Savannah, Georgia, typifies a garden environment. As one of the country's oldest cities, Savannah was built on an urban grid that dates to pre-Colonial times. James Olgethorpe, the original town planner, envisioned a series of squares that would provide a compact, functional, and beautiful streetscape. Some of these became town squares with open park spaces in the middle.

Savannah's urban DNA was a no-nonsense, straightforward succession of squares that look boring and mundane on paper. However, with the addition of brick Georgian architecture, cobblestone streets, and lush Spanish moss draped from maturing oak trees, Savannah's urban feeling produces something special and far from the ordinary.

Savannah (from the river to Forsyth Park) features wrought-iron masterpieces, trolleys, and some of the most spectacular fountains and squares seen anywhere. There are sitting nooks and miniparks on almost every corner. The setting is like a movie, and Savannah has been the backdrop for many films. Regardless of the surreal environment provided, Savannah is a real place with real people.

The city boasts its main town green: Forsyth Park. This oasis in the center of much of the urbanized portion of the city is surrounded by fine homes and features an expansive lawn with impressive fountains. Many residents are drawn to the footpaths to walk their dog, hone their soccer-playing skills, or relax on the large green under an old oak tree. Thousands of tourists come here to see the city's stunning beauty.

> *Many other urban American neighborhoods look, feel, and act a lot like Savannah. Some are so similar that, without looking at the local vegetation and the nuances of the local architecture, it would be hard to know that you are not in Georgia. Every city has a Savannah—lush, calming, and in the middle of the vibrant urban area. The following urbs, although far from representing a comprehensive list, are excellent examples.*

OLD LOUISVILLE— "VICTORIA"

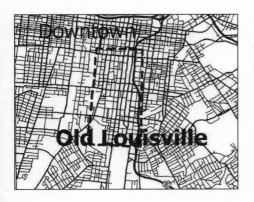

Old Louisville promotes itself as the "largest Victorian neighborhood in America." It could be right. This urb, just south of downtown Louisville, is impressive when considering that its huge land mass could be a separate city of its own. Even more impressive is its stunning natural and architectural beauty.

Several gigantic Victorian mansions line wide boulevards with lush green medians. Also offered are historic duplexes and row homes, both of which are graceful and extravagantly adorned. Scaffolding is also a prominent feature on many buildings, with eager painters and carpenters dangling from the temporary steel rods, trying to erase the ravages of time. The level of preservation and attention to detail is apparent, not unlike Beacon

Hill in Boston, central Savannah, or the Battery in Charleston. In many ways Old Louisville is superior. For instance, every Garden Urb is expected to have shady trees, but Old Louisville is more like a dense urban forest. Tall trees are striking centerpieces for roundabouts and wide, grassy medians. Trees also frame grand residential boulevards with their extensive canopies, sharply contrasting with the nearby asphalt-covered downtown. Shade, especially apparent in the summertime, makes this neighborhood a popular respite from the muggy Kentucky heat.

Old Louisville is also a walker's paradise. Wide sidewalks allow people to pass each other while admiring elaborate fountains, Victorian-style public art, and lavish landscaping consisting of hedgerows and wrought-iron fences. Dog walkers emerge from narrow back alleys and converge with joggers and baby strollers in the aptly named Central Park. This is where pre–Kentucky Derby parties and art festivals make the otherwise sedate atmosphere an exhilarating experience. Bikepaths, willow trees,

Stately Victorian homes, all with front porches (some with grand columns), wrought-iron decorative fences, established hedgerows, and historic fountains predominate in Old Louisville.

and water features enable residents to reflect serenely. Central Park and the surrounding treed streets are one of America's greatest urban residential experiences.

Adding to the quaintness are several of mom-and-pop shops, including groceries, specialty boutiques, antiques stores, dry cleaners, and restaurants scattered throughout the urb. This is the "charming" address for the entire Louisville region. With the active neighborhood association's passion for historic preservation, Old Louisville keeps the momentum high, offering a calming, beautiful urban atmosphere, with charm and elegance, making life here a pleasure.

MOUNT VERNON, BALTIMORE— *"OLD EUROPE"*

Many people fantasize about moving to a beautiful, grand, old European city, complete with an active sidewalk culture, al fresco dining, and extravagant architecture. For most Americans, life in urban Europe will remain a fantasy; however, life in Baltimore's Mount Vernon may be just as satisfying.

As the grande dame of Baltimore's urbs, Mt. Vernon combines the best of urban Amsterdam, London, and Paris with a bit of a hilly English fishing village. People walk to urban grocery stores with goods that spill out onto the sidewalk. They talk to neighbors on front stoops and paint watercolors in ancient parks. Mt. Vernon is a good example of a highly polished Garden Urb.

Although other urbs hope to achieve this level of aesthetic perfection, Mt. Vernon has a major advantage because of its truly spectacular architecture. The urb is home to Baltimore's quintessential three- to five-story vintage row houses and carriage homes. Architectural styles are varied and marvelously preserved. Textbook Renaissance Revival, Beaux Arts,

The Mount Vernon sidewalk scene is unapologetically ultrasophisticated.

and Georgian homes are well maintained and showcase the appropriate details of the period they represent. Even the streetlamps and their supporting posts look as if they are colonial originals.

The grid layout, an irregular, hilly "Montmartre" style, is also superior. It provides intentional views of statues and tall monuments, each standing just at the right spot. Tall church steeples, statues, and important buildings line the beautiful Charles Street corridor, adding to the European ambience while providing a cozy feel.

The grid also makes room for European-style parks of all sizes. Grand squares and smaller pocket parks are available for reading, chatting, and just "being." Mature trees line up just so along the streets, contributing a peaceful element for the stressed-out. The quality of Mt. Vernon's parks equals any European showplace.

Urban paradise is revealed in the active sidewalk culture. Sidewalks are packed with pedestrians, joggers, merchants, and random urban revelers. The walks are wide enough to accommodate strollers, readers, chatters, painters, dog walkers, architecture aficionados, and people watchers.

Mount Vernon's personality is best understood by hanging out at any of the many urban cafés and coffee shops. Residents read their newspapers, sip lattes, and crunch biscotti just like in many other places. The Mount Vernon difference is the context in which these activities are performed. It is an urban setting with architectural significance and urban beauty. Outside activities, no matter how mundane, are automatically (although unintentionally) fashionable because of the setting.

As Baltimore's cultural and entertainment center, Mount Vernon provides traditional and alternative plays, period and contemporary art museums, dancing at nightclubs, soaking up jazz, and taking pictures at the George Washington monument. This urb provides one of the most desirable Euro-style garden experiences.

QUAWPAW QUARTER, LITTLE ROCK—"URBAN GARDEN PARADISE"

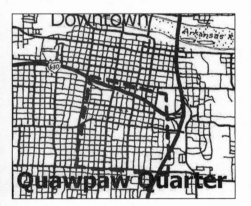

Arkansas's capital (and only real) city has fewer than 200,000 residents. It looks and feels much larger since its center city offers the same kinds of urban amenities found in places five times its size. Little Rock is coming into its own, and this is particularly true in its "Quawpaw Quarter."

Quawpaw begins at the south side of the rapid-fire emerging downtown. The neighborhood is a large historic district resembling a mix of Savannah and New Orleans' garden districts. Several historic neighborhoods make up this urb, including the MacArthur Park Historic District, the Governor's Mansion Historic District, and the residential area just south of downtown Little Rock. The urb features tree trunks wider than cars, beautifully preserved architecture, charming parks, and quaint churches.

Quawpaw has exquisitely restored homes, but there are still a few fixer-uppers waiting for elbow grease. New redevelopment projects add to the residential mix, including the conversion of an old schoolhouse into apartments and some aboveground residences discovered in an emerging malternative corridor. If this kind of neighborhood were in Los Angeles, Boston, or Miami, songs would be written about it.

Visitors can view some of the interiors of important historic mansions or take a group tour to admire the structures from the sidewalk. Art museums are housed in pre–Civil War houses. Quawpaw's antebellum architecture is so gorgeous that it has become a tourist destination.

While Quawpaw attracts tourists, it is far from a tourist trap. Hungry residents can choose between shopping at a local, full-service grocery store or walking to downtown Little Rock's hip River Market for unique culinary items or something to eat by the Arkansas River. In addition to its own unique beauty, Quawpaw offers brilliant downtown skyline views.

HISTORIC EAST NASHVILLE—"THE REAL MUSIC 'CITY'"

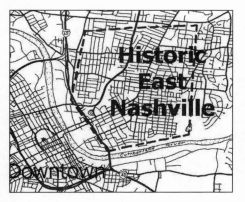

Just a ten-minute walk up a hill, east of the new stadium that is home to the Tennessee Titans professional football team, sits Historic East Nashville. This is the best urban system of neighborhoods in this sprawling metropolis. Greater Nashville is a very suburban region, having developed primarily from the 1950s to the present. As a result, many "urban" Nashvillians have never been on this hill. It lacks freeways and is beyond the sight of the multitudes choosing to live in south and west Nashville.

Quietly, slowly, Historic East Nashville is experiencing nothing short of a residential revolution. People here are passionate about their quality neighborhoods (Lockeland Springs, Bailey-Cora Howe, Eastwood, East End, Boscobel Heights, and Edgefield, to name only a few). All of these areas comprise first-ring suburbs, housing a mix of middle- and upper-middle-class professionals at the turn of the century. The combination of these old neighborhoods creates the largest intact historic housing stock in Nashville.

The urb provides residents with rare sidewalks, narrow streets, front porches, and old, traditional architecture. Homes here are a combination of large Victorian estates, working-class shotgun houses, and other tidy styles. Regardless of the houses' size, the neighborhood offers a cheerful gingerbread setting. Nearly all of the homes feature ornate trim and vivid, historically accurate primary and pastel exterior colors. It is impossible to find an urban environment like this in Music City.

Although white picket fences have not been sanctioned officially as the urb's icon or brand, the entire area seems to have embraced them. They line many front yards and look like they belong, not like fake add-ons. The combination of the fences, architectural diversity, and a mature tree canopy is irresistible for many suburbanites who are seeking a

White columns and original wood siding are typical of houses. Picket fences, the unofficial icon of Historic East Nashville, delineate many front yards.

real neighborhood instead of a cookie-cutter home in the nearby sub-urban communities of Mt. Juliet, Hendersonville, and all the others.

Residents know their neighbors, hold crime watches, form commu-nity organizations, and have Sunday picnics together. New residents drawn to the historic architecture become preservation fanatics as a re-sult of their unorthodox real estate decisions. Folks here love visiting their shops, walking along the tree-lined streets, and talking with their neighbors. It's evident how proud they are to be here.

Today the area still has limited urban services compared to most other urbs of this type. There are few large-scale retail opportunities, so you need a car to survive here. But more neighborhood services could locate here, and will, with increased interest and momentum.

This urb is exciting because it is so newly appreciated—so different from the more "fashionable" areas west of the Cumberland River that enjoy the lion's share of the region's income and population. However, the west-river bumper-to-bumper traffic, generic strip malls, bland sub-divisions, and multitude of parking lots—so desired in the previous century—is passé. No area in the city can match the much more civil, beautiful, and urbane Historic East Nashville.

In the coming years, Historic East Nashville will continue to trans-form into a place that will be home to anyone and everyone—from low-income residents to urban country music stars. All it will take is for people to discover what's over the hill.

GERMAN VILLAGE, COLUMBUS, OHIO— *"A GERMAN VILLAGE"*

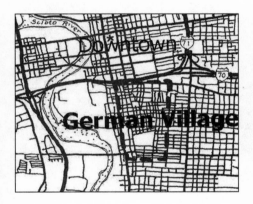

German Village's rich history fuels its excellent neighbor-hood quality of today. In-habited by Germans fleeing wars and famine in the early and mid-1800s, the homes and businesses constructed here resembled what was left behind in the old coun-try. During the world wars, German-Americans angli-cized all of the street names, changing Schiller Park to Washington Park to avoid the discrimination and anti-German bias of the time.

In the 1950s, with urban flight to suburban Columbus in full force, a combination of inner-belt freeway construction and urban renewal projects claimed the northern section of this unique neighborhood. Spurred by this devastation, urban activists made sure it didn't happen again. If not for a few native residents seeing the worth in the small cot-tages and brick-paved streets, German Village could have been just an-other flattened area paved over in the name of progress. Today, it is the largest privately funded historic district in the entire country. It is also a magnificent urban neighborhood.

German Village is Columbus's biggest tourist attraction. On any weekend, out-of-towners looking to be "wowed" in the center of

Ohio always are. German Village hosts "Oktoberfest," a grand celebration of everything German, a locally renowned "Haus and Garten
Tour," and cozy bookstores and coffee haus-es. The neighborhood
does an excellent job of emphasizing its German heritage, with the
preserved architecture, the language on signs, and the overall European ambience.

German Village has mostly single-family historic residences, along
with a few small apartment complexes. Neighborhoods to the south
and east, including Merion Village and Schumacher Place, benefit
greatly from the spillover of German Village's success. Newcomers to
Columbus, especially preservationist buffs, are drawn automatically to
this impeccably mothballed neighborhood in the Midwest.

SOULARD, ST. LOUIS—"NEW ORLEANS, MISSOURI"

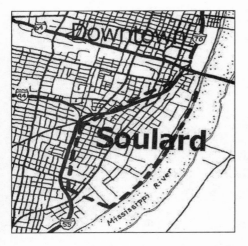

By visual standards, Soulard, just south of downtown St. Louis, is a quintessential Garden Urb. Soulard is also unusual; it has an eclectic, funky, and celebratory air not found in most similarly quaint-looking urbs. Perhaps the reason for this is that it used to be a part of Louisiana before the famous "purchase" in 1803. Its French connection has created a New Orleans look, especially in the way it mirrors the Faubourg Marigny neighborhood just east of the French Quarter. Soulard even hosts one of the largest Mardi Gras celebrations in the United States outside of New Orleans.

Its residences are remarkable, dominated by grand Victorians, Italianate working-class structures, carriage houses, block-long row homes, and old-fashioned duplexes located on the rolling, tree-lined knolls. The predominant building material is red brick, so the structures blend together in an authentic urban village setting. Soulard enjoys a diverse and active sidewalk culture, with families strolling infants, singles walking dogs, twenty-somethings rollerblading, and older generations walking with canes. Walking here is special because of the colorful flower beds and tiny, welcoming minifront yards.

If you like to walk, you're never too far from services like miniature neighborhood grocery stores, specialty boutique shops, and even medical offices located in an old corner building. Soulard is also home of the original Budweiser Brewery. Impressively huge, the brewery blends in amazingly well. Budweiser helped to form and still contributes to the health of the urb. Many employees lived and worked in the same area, and some still do.

Soulard's residents may have completely different types of structures on each side of their homes.

It's not surprising that Soulard has a slew of taverns where a cold keg of Bud can be tapped on demand. To go along with the beer, there are plenty of restaurants scattered throughout, including local carryouts, pastry shops, diners, bakeries, and even fine dining. Fresh food is at home here, too. Soulard hosts one of St. Louis's oldest and most famous outdoor food shopping experience in the Soulard Market. This is unusual, as so many public markets typically are found in Postindustrial Urbs.

The hundreds of thousands of people who fled inner-city St. Louis, and perhaps those who fled Soulard itself, now probably wonder why they left. This urb has evolved into an open-minded, fun-loving place for people who want an urban garden ambience with a soulful, eclectic, and slightly off-center lifestyle.

ROOSEVELT, PHOENIX—"DESERT GARDEN"

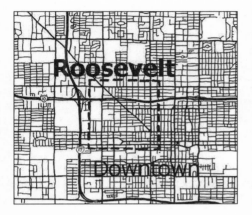

Hot, dry, and Arizona, are not usually adjectives used to describe a lush garden environment. Just northwest of downtown Phoenix, Roosevelt offers a rare opportunity for people who want the same kind of urban setting and lifestyle as exists in the East, while enjoying the comforts and beauty of a desert environment. Although not as humid or as leafy as Savannah, Roosevelt still has the qualities of small-town life, even though it's surrounded by a big city.

Tidy, old-style houses front wide sidewalks just like "back East."

Graceful, tall, and perfectly spaced palm trees line the planting strips between the streets and sidewalks. Historic houses, mostly desert bungalows, are welcoming and charming. There is even significant infill development, including condominiums and apartments with architectural detailing compatible with that of the historic single-family homes.

Roosevelt stands out because of its close proximity to employment and shopping opportunities in downtown Phoenix, just a few blocks away. For many people living here, commutes are virtually stress-free, whether on foot or by bicycle, bus, or even car. Roosevelt residents who work downtown choose when to battle the increasingly clogged Phoenix freeway system.

The irony of such a charming place to live in such an unlikely city makes Roosevelt a model urb for the rest of Phoenix, not to mention other desert cities such as Las Vegas, Tucson, and Albuquerque.

OREGON, DAYTON— "GEORGETOWN IN OHIO"

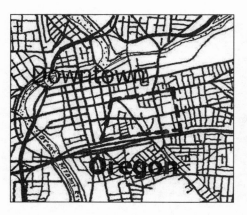

As described in chapter 4, downtown Dayton is one of America's up-and-coming Postindustrial Urbs. Its sleek architecture, featuring the metallic hues and substantial masonry of the bygone industrial era, is a magnet for urbanites. Immediately south and east, adjacent to downtown, the Oregon District provides a jolting contrast.

The first jolt is a brick-and-wrought iron welcome monument with "Oregon" etched in concrete. You know you're entering an altogether different place, but its close proximity to gritty downtown is unexpected. This marker's historic design hints at the surprises farther inside the urb.

Brick sidewalks and huge deciduous trees give the area a warm,

"Oregon" marks the transition to edgy "postindustrial" downtown Dayton.

homey feeling. Historic two-story brick homes with tiny front yards are filled with perennials, Japanese maple trees, and other simple, elegant landscaping elements. This neighborhood is one of Dayton's picture postcard opportunities because it is a Midwestern version of the residential back streets of Georgetown in Washington, D.C.

Oregon is where many suburbanites throughout the Miami Valley get their urban fix. The otherwise sleepy Oregon neighborhood satisfies them with the unique businesses centered on Fifth Street, which features a charming mallternative with some of Dayton's best restaurants and bars, specialty shops, and boutiques. Fifth Street is also a great place for a casual stroll, window shopping, and meeting friends.

Oregon living is now obviously at a premium due to the proliferation of "coming soon" signs posted on vacant lots throughout the urb. New homes are being constructed, using "Oregon-approved" architecture that closely mimics the forms and styles of existing single-family homes.

NEAR EAST LEXINGTON—*"THE INNER CITY OF TREES"*

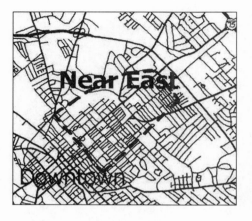

Inner-city Lexington forgot it was an inner city. The neighborhoods in the immediate downtown are immaculate, stunning examples of what a city without a freeway cutting through its middle can look like. Without big roads, the trees survived, historic homes still stand, and the downtown and surrounding Lexington neighborhoods have never gone out of style. This is true especially in the hilly residential neighborhoods just east of downtown.

There are several tiny historic neighborhoods here, almost too many to mention. In spite of some of them being less than two or three

blocks wide, they are significant parts that make a bold statement when taken as a whole.

On the Near East Side, especially when leaves are full on the trees, you'd never know you were in a city of any size. Quaint streets, some along the slopes of the rolling landscape, create nooks and crannies, hiding little homes where zoning would never allow them to be built today. Some residential enclaves front impressive tree-lined boulevards; others sit inside courtyards with large greens. Most are on narrow streets forming a traditional street grid. The variety of streets here creates an ambience that is unmistakably Lexington.

Other than its beauty, the best aspect of the Near East Side is its direct access to the cultural, employment, and entertainment opportunities just steps away in downtown Lexington. This urb offers a hidden world that isn't really hidden at all. This is, unbelievably, the inner city.

SPRINGFIELD, JACKSONVILLE— "IOWA IN FLORIDA"

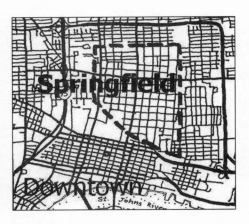

Central city Jacksonville, not far from the beach and on a shimmering harbor, has all the trappings of typical Florida: sand, sun, and fun. Yet, Jacksonville is different from Miami or Tampa in that it offers (almost unbelievably) a small-town experience similar to what you can expect to find in the Midwest. Welcome to Springfield.

Springfield has what look like Iowa farmhouses everywhere. If not for the palm trees and sandy roads, it would be hard to tell this is Florida. This urb also features some of the best park spaces in the South, especially the wide-open and beautiful Confederate Park, an extensive green belt where picnics, socials, and frisbee throwing are still popular.

Springfield is different from the other Garden Urbs in this chapter because it's a work in progress. Even though its neighborhoods are beautiful, many homes and businesses are still suffering from the mass exodus to the suburbs. Springfield has lost many people over the last several decades, but new development is filling in the vacant properties of years past. A transformation sparked by new interest and repopulation is happening in this area—contractors are very busy with rehabilitation work, and neighborhood tours are generating interest and pride. Springfield is experiencing the kind of momentum that reinvestment and a little elbow grease can provide. Its streets and public spaces are becoming cleaner, safer, and more desirable as a result of the obvious hard work of longtime residents and enthusiastic newcomers.

A cornfield and tractor could be just behind this house—but this is urban Florida.

The greatest momentum is happening along Springfield's main commercial core, centered on Main Street, with its great view of downtown Jacksonville. Although not a full-fledged mallternative, Main Street has the potential to draw the kinds of neighborhood services that can benefit the locals and even beckon people off the beaches to experience urban life in Jacksonville.

FINDING THE GARDEN URB(S) IN *YOUR* CITY

Those searching for a Garden Urb in any city will find that they are perhaps the easiest urb to locate. Garden Urbs are likely to have all of the following:

- A location on the fastest-growing side during the early 1900s. (If this is unknown, try to determine the oldest side of the city and start there.)
- Trees—and lots of them, regardless of climate and species.
- Large, grand parks.
- Antiques stores; the traditional, quaint architecture calls for antiques stores.
- Several homes on the National Register of Historic Places. Plaques proudly displayed on the front or side of these structures make them easy to find.
- Find out where the bankers, doctors, and lawyers lived during the early 1900s—that area is probably a Garden Urb.

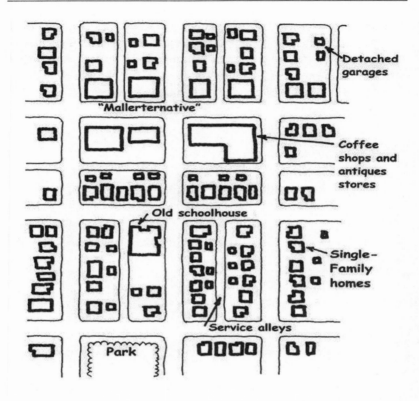

The figure above depicts a typical garden urb. These urbs have the tightest street grid, with tree-lined sidewalks and service alleys behind single-family homes. Most have "quainter than quaint" mallternatives that serve the neighborhood and act as the local social gathering place. Garden Urbs always have the lushest, most beautiful parks of at least one square block (or, often, much larger).

Do Garden Urbs look and feel like a place where you'd like to live? Does a lush, slower-paced urban lifestyle full of flowers and fountains fit your personality? If so, you can use the information learned in this chapter to find a Garden Urb of your own. But, before you answer, consider the next chapter, which features "Eclectic Urbs," with an interesting mix of urban elements.

6

Eclectic Urbs

Every city has a Greenwich Village

You Are an Eclectic Urbanite If You . . .

- Consider yourself a "weirdo" and want to be surrounded by other "weirdos."
- Hate conforming and places that conform—especially those with preferred "color palettes," most notably beige and brown.
- Prefer to live where "strange" is normal and "normal" is strange.
- Choose to live among the most diverse neighbors in the city.
- Appreciate having an eclectic array of visual and performing arts nearby.
- Want many local choices of, or have a desire to live around, a diversity of architectural styles.
- Opt to live in what is usually the most innovative area of the city.
- Get bored easily and need a lot of urban energy.
- Like change and revolt against neighborhood stagnation.
- Are expressive and need to feel free to be able to express that freedom in a variety of situations.
- Have diverse hobbies and interests and want to live in a neighborhood where you can learn from many of the city's most openly creative residents.

CALLING DIVERSITY

Some urbs stand out because they feature a little bit of everything possible in a city—an eclectic mix of what is found in the best urban neighborhoods. These "Eclectic Urbs" draw such interest because they have pieces of each kind of urb, including architectural styles, quaint and quiet enclaves, and roaring districts full of high energy. Due to their diversity of residents with a wide variety of interests, Eclectic Urbs often represent a city's overall image and composite personality.

Because they offer variety, Eclectic Urbs are a bit difficult to pin down. Many different kinds of activities are offered, and they attract different types of people. As a result, these areas emit a complex variety of urban vitality, events, moods, rhythms, and personalities that are always changing. Eclectic Urbs are special because they offer their own unique brand of urban energy, and no two are exactly alike.

Loosely speaking, Eclectic Urbs are "funky," a vague and overused word. Nevertheless, funky is the perfect adjective to describe such places. *Webster's Dictionary* defines funky as "having an earthy quality that is characteristic of the blues," and "outlandishly and often humorously vulgar." Regarding the description of funky urban places, *Webster's* misses the mark. A funky urban neighborhood is too complex to be summed up in one or two phrases.

FUNKY DEFINED

"Funky" is a combination of design features, people, activities, art, colors, behavior, functions, lifestyles, and other components that exist in a place that is skewed, often far left of center. Since the meaning of "normal" is individual, levels of funk in a place can be interpreted in just as many ways. Regardless, Eclectic Urbs have specific funky qualities that, analyzed individually, can explain the total funky feeling and help those seeking a special lifestyle to identify it when they experience it. "Funky" places have:

A Diversity of People

If you walked into an urban coffee shop packed with customers, and most people were either yuppies, or all students, or all bohemians, the ambience wouldn't be very funky. A business whose patrons comprise only one group can be fun, but a funky business might include blue-haired women, a businessman crunching numbers, deaf people signing in a frenzy, a drag queen and her loud yackety friends, a Rastafarian, a businessman, a paraplegic sipping through a straw, a soccer mom and her two daughters, a preacher bearing a life-size cross, a group of rappers rapping, and average Joes and Janes all sitting outside under a bubble blower—now *that's funky*! The funkiness of a place also increases tremendously if diverse types "mix" and do not "group" too much.

Personal Expression

Urbs are funkiest when their residents don't get too caught up in Madison Avenue trends, but express their own tastes and styles instead. Whoever they want to be today is possible. Places are not very funky if everyone seems to be wearing the same color, looks the same, talks the same, acts the same, and *is* the same. Funky places encourage people to express themselves. Whatever you want to look like—whatever suits your style, regardless of whether it's in style, is funky.

Expressionism doesn't just mean how people look. Verbal, political, cultural, and social expression is important, too. Eclectic places are normally the center of political protests, alternative theater, poetry writings and readings, culinary creations, and special community events that would never be held in suburbia.

Art Overflowing

Not just art—but the kind that makes you look twice, or look long, for whatever reason. Most people have visited art galleries that are not inherently funky but uncomfortably stuffy. Eclectic Urbs' art galleries feature classic oils one month and "live" human statues the next. Art variety encourages an unpredictability that makes it funky.

Public art that creates mystery and intrigue is especially funky. For instance, a multicolored, pastel-striped zebra with a monochromatic magenta leprechaun on its back is funky. If that zebra and leprechaun are on a giant mural in the center of a space—it creates an over-the-top energy. Funky places are normally the most thought-provoking places with the widest variety of art.

Interesting Architecture

The funkiest places have a mix of architectural styles, colors, materials, and building sizes. As explained in chapter 2, buildings harness urban energy. Different sizes, shapes, and colors of buildings are necessary to satisfy discriminating urban weirdos who want to live in the midst of urban energy with a distinct local flavor. Diverse architecture is one of the most important contributors in creating eclectic, exciting, unusual, and endearing city neighborhoods. For this reason, people who live in nonfunky places such as suburban subdivisions and want the opposite living experience will appreciate Eclectic Urbs.

Retro or Futuristic Building Interiors

The insides of buildings also contribute to funk. "Normal" places with normal interiors feature the current decorating style, or perhaps a style that may be a few years old. Commonly used paint colors, wallpaper, furniture, and fixtures that can be found in strip malls or fast-food restaurants are the opposite of funky. Funky urbs often feature innovative, futuristic interiors like shiny metals, or retro 1940s, 1890s, or 1970s, or an interpretation of the twenty-second century (or any period). As long as the interior looks "past" or "future," and past and future are unique, it's funky. Since trends repeat themselves, it's sometimes hard to differentiate retro from futuristic. It doesn't matter. Funky interiors are funky as long as they aren't what's going on today.

Truly Special Special Events

Ordinary urbs lacking the vision to create extraordinary occasions, traditions, and events usually must copy others' creative innovations. There are dozens of jazz fests around the country, even in places where, as a musical genre, jazz is out of context. Ribfests abound from Vermont to Oregon. Countless urban neighborhoods feature "A Dickens

Christmas" as their holiday special event. Many urban neighborhoods couldn't be any less creative. Events are important because they feed on activity and spawn vitality, moods, and expression (urban energy). Nationally unique events are locally important because they are place-definers, showcasing that area as being different from the rest.

Worldwide, places that host one-of-a-kind special events have become famous, and their customs have become household names. Pamplona, Spain's running of the bulls cannot be duplicated. It seems that almost every city now has a local version of a Mardi Gras, working hard to match New Orleans' continued fame, instead of producing an event that would bring local notoriety. No running of the bulls can equal Pamplona's, and a spin-off of Mardi Gras could never beat the New Orleans version. The funkiest of urbs have truly singular special events, such as "The Day of the Dog," "Celebration of the Sun, "World Cow Dance," or "International Kazoo Parade"—anything that's distinctively different.

Traditional events, parades, and carnivals ordinarily are left to other types of urbs. The funkiest Eclectic Urbs insist on making their own bold statements with mass celebrations that would even attract tourists from New Orleans or Spain to book a hotel room for a week. More important, funked-up special events are an economic development machine, attracting the attention of potential new residents looking to live in the most special, fun, and exciting urb possible.

"Strange" Behavior

Think of an everyday behavior or tradition that has become specific to an urban area. South Beach (Miami) features a twenty-four-hour stream of cruising and rollerblading down the art deco architecture along Oceanfront Drive. Downtown Detroit is increasingly becoming famous for its techno music electronic dance festivals. Columbus's Short North's special offering is participating in public political satires (as in its "Do-Dah Parade"). All of these behaviors are perfectly normal in the context of each urb, but they would be considered funky anywhere else.

Funky behaviors are not limited to the masses; they also can include surprises like seeing a group of people dressed up like Coneheads or rabbits singing for change. Local behavior is considered funky if it is impromptu, strange, and offers wonderful or thought-provoking diversions from the normalcy of everyday life. Funky behaviors are live art forms, a part of what makes city life interesting. People who live in funky urbs consider it a responsibility to add to the variety of life by contributing their special version of funky behavior to the local street life and energy.

"A Thing"

Urbs that have one or more "things" are eclectic. In this context, "things" are local icons that are so special, they are beyond definition. One thing is good, more than one thing is better. They can be statues, bridges, long-standing businesses, or anything at all that adds to the local sense of place because they are specific to a particular urb. They can be classic, like Greenwich Village's Washington Square Arch, or beloved restaurants like South Philly's famous-for-Philly-cheesesteak eateries. They can be as simple as a singular light pole that has been embellished with hubcaps and mannequins. A litmus test for qualifying as a "thing" is whether the neighborhood would be upset if it were removed or threatened. Funky places with many funky things are often quality living experiences or places where locals feel extremely attached to their neighborhoods. The thing becomes part of the identity of the urb.

There are many other aspects of funky. Eclectic Urbs are always different, and you might have your own criteria. The urbs described in this chapter will help you hone this concept.

GREENWICH VILLAGE—THE ORIGINAL ECLECTIC URB

Although natives of Lower Manhattan's Greenwich Village quickly point out that their neighborhood has lost a good bit of funkiness and eclecticism over the decades, this urb is the birthplace of many of the important eclectic elements enjoyed in every American city. Greenwich Village was perhaps at its most eclectic in the 1960s, an era that featured beatniks snapping their fingers (instead of clapping) in applause at a far-out poetry reading. It attracted artists from all over the world,

Greenwich Village is special because of its uninhibited spirit, found in its architecture and signage.

many starving happily on the sidewalks. Greenwich Village is also famous as the birthplace of an important human rights movement, with police riots at the Stonewall Inn that sparked a worldwide civil rights following for gay people. Adding to the area's eclectic history, New York University plays an important role in maintaining a local youthful outlook where politics and social issues continue to be classified as experimental.

Greenwich Village is also the original home of "bohemians," the American version of a gypsy from Bohemia. This wide-ranging people group usually includes anyone outside the mainstream: freethinkers, artists, and highly creative people of all kinds and those who practice unbridled expressionism. Hippies and the antiwar protesters during the Korean and Vietnam era are often included under the bohemian label, although Greenwich Village has long been associated with a specific hippie population as well.

For most of the second half of the 1900s, Greenwich Village and cultural innovation were one and the same. Famous songwriters, musi-

Sidewalks still become art galleries because "they are there."

cians, and actors (too many to name) got their start in the local bars and nightclubs. Avant-garde playwrights have made their home here, far from mainstream theater productions. Chefs have cooked and lived here. Creative types from the world over have dreamed of life in Greenwich Village. Many people like the idea of being surrounded by unceasing creativity and cutting-edge ideas.

Even today, from one eclectic street corridor to the next, you never know what to expect. Run-of-the-mill grocery stores and delis, hip coffee shops, alternative sports bars, predominately gay sing-along piano cabarets, ethnic restaurants, chain drugstores, expensive art galleries, cheap knickknack stores, doggie bakeries, dry cleaners—you name it, and Greenwich Village probably has it. In spite of having lost much of the activism and hard-core bohemianism of the past, Greenwich Village remains funky, especially compared to much of the rest of urban America.

Today's more sedate Greenwich Village maintains a spontaneous rhythm and energy that can be felt on the sidewalks. The pace is a mix of small town and metropolis. Its history is established and proud, making it an interesting place to write about. The urb is still revered for its contribution to world society and culture and has become a model for hundreds of other urban communities. Perhaps, even as some of the extreme funk and counterculture have become mainstream here, the idea of Greenwich Village and its energy has just begun to be understood and appreciated in heartland urbs.

> *You don't have to live in Greenwich Village to have an Eclectic Urban atmosphere and lifestyle; they can be found in every city. The rest of this chapter features examples of places where people enjoy Eclectic Urban living.*

THE SHORT NORTH, COLUMBUS, OHIO—"ART IN YOUR FACE"

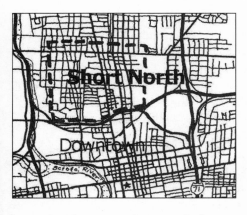

"The Short North" was a phrase coined by the Columbus Police Department whose members frequented the area adjacent to downtown. They didn't have time to utter any longer place description because of the frequency of police calls to this high-crime and prostitution haven during the 1970s and early 1980s. The area had lost a significant population and a huge number of businesses to the suburbs, making it one of Columbus's premier ghettos—a gateway of embarrassment between downtown and the Ohio State University campus.

Something magical happened in the 1980s. An unusual mix of people, including bohemians, gay people, urban developers, architects, entrepreneurs, and an onslaught of other urban "weirdos" took up residence in some of the area's dilapidated houses. They risked being pedestrians on otherwise foreboding streets, fixed up businesses, and took down boards from the windows. Urban developers and rehabilitation specialists with a dream and a prayer began investing in buildings and properties that many of their suburban counterparts considered to be lost causes.

Over time, highly inventive people caught the fever and became new neighbors, producing an infectious, creative atmosphere few places have ever known. Painters, hairstylists, bartenders, sculptors, glass-blowers, photographers, landscapers, architects, carpenters, shopkeep-ers, and others began working magic on the blighted structures and streets. This neighborhood has become unquestionably Columbus's—and the entire state of Ohio's—most interesting, exciting, and eclectic places.

Rapid-fire change from ghetto to fabulous happened in less than ten years, accompanied by ambitious public and private improvements. During the 1980s, preservation and restoration were concentrated on historic buildings facing Columbus's major thoroughfare, High Street. Drug havens turned into five-star restaurants; crumbling facades were saved, cleaned, and painted vibrant colors; and chic art replaced moth-balled building interiors. The transformation was amazing.

During the 1990s, a major streetscape improvement encouraged pre-viously extinct pedestrians, window shoppers, and high energy. Appro-priately designed infill apartment buildings added hundreds of new residents to the neighborhood in many locations along and near High Street. In the early 2000s, more interesting new development and posi-tive change continue to be going strong—all because the Short North found its niche—*in-your-face art*.

Although many American urbs have art as a theme, The Short North takes it to the nth degree. Spontaneous and funky art is around every corner, featuring icons such as the "hubcap pole," scattered with an ever-evolving collage of old hubcaps painted pink, sky blue, and orange (even a dangling bicycle); rainbow-colored awnings; and innovative wall murals. Spontaneity, color, and alternative art contrast sharply with the rest of otherwise conservative Midwestern Columbus. If the Short North could talk, it would say, "Bam!" and "Take that!" But it's too re-fined to be overtly rude—after all, it is officially known as "The Fabu-lous Short North," with the emphasis on the first syllable in fabulous.

The Short North does a great job of advertising itself as uniquely

A twist on "American Gothic" *painted on a building wall.*

askew, attracting similar kinds of people from all over the Midwest and the East Coast. Its signature brand is Mona Lisa, and she is always shown in a sideways orientation, making it clear that few things should be considered right-side up or "normal" here. "Sideways Lisa," as many refer to her, is everywhere, but the largest version is included in a mural on the Reality Theater just off High Street. A late addition to the local skewing of famous art is the upside-down version of "American Gothic" on a blank wall along High Street.

Quickly challenging the painted public art, The Short North recently constructed a series of twenty arches that hug the street during the day and provide a sea of light at night. The lit globes change colors and "dance" down the street with each event and season. Columbus was known as the arch city in the late 1890s, and may regain the title when these new structures gain more notoriety.

The area's varied public art has attracted art of other kinds as well. Galleries predominate on and near High Street, and for fifteen years, the

Off-site billboards help steer outlanders to their adopted mallternative.

locals have hosted "Gallery Hop," one of the most electric urban experiences. Gallery Hop is held the first Saturday night of the month, year-round, rain or shine.

The Gallery Hop is a spectacle of walking people-watchers. It attracts every kind of person, including those wearing suits, monochromatic black clothing, fancy formal attire, "drag" gear, or just a tank top and jeans. People "hop" from one art gallery to the next among spinning disc jockeys, pan flute players, jugglers, jazz soloists, high school bands, human statues, mimes, and other self-designated "freaks." Freaks with purple hair and full-body tattoos, suburban moms strolling wide-eyed kids, and just-back-from-the-show sophisticates all look each other over in a friendly and welcoming way. Many people get "hooked" on Gallery Hop, and this event has a lot to do with the Short North's enduring success.

Even though pedestrian energy skyrockets and peaks at Gallery Hop, during any hour of the day the streets of The Short North provide a stimulating experience full of human interaction and a bit of mystery. You never know what characters or weird events will come along many of the area's wonderfully strange yet sophisticated urban corridors. Being a pedestrian here means adding to the energy of High Street, creating the perfect "high" for truly eclectic city lovers. Unusual encounters happen day and night, including sidewalk interactions with people from all backgrounds, races, and philosophies. High Street is a creative American melting pot.

A stroll here tantalizes the senses with a fusion of smells (among the most interesting, cakes baking at the nearby bread factory) sounds (buses roaring, laughter and chitchat of excited locals), and sights (tongue rings, peculiar, but wonderful art mixed with stiff collars). For people seeking an alternative version of urban energy, there is nothing quite like High Street.

Other kinds of fun include eating out at one of several excellent restaurants. Many people enjoy dressing up for dinner in the otherwise ultracasual Short North in honor of a special occasion. The Short North is home to Columbus's creative set: three alternative theaters where the daring, funny, and controversial coexist. High-energy dance clubs, slick martini bars, and local hangouts that have been around since the 1960s welcome diversity. The Short North is one of the best alternative high-energy urbs found anywhere.

NORTHSHORE, CHATTANOOGA—"OUTDOOR SPORTS; MANHATTAN CULTURE"

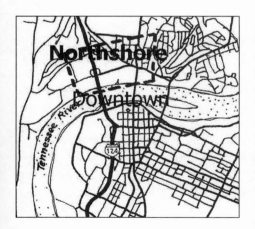

Northshore is a sparkling example of the best of what southern city life can offer. Its street activity, scenery, and individuality make it hard to believe such a place could exist in the "sleepy South." It's electric and funky as it is picturesque and diverse. It is further enhanced by being the hub of Chattanooga culture, including a strong arts, music, and theater scene. The Chattanooga Theater Center on the banks of the Tennessee River is not far from the outdoor music amphitheater and the hip Frazier Avenue art gallery corridor.

A lot of urbs have art and culture. Northshore creates a niche by mixing highbrow activities with edgy, thriving outdoor sports. This place has more mountain bikers, boaters, rowers, cross-country runners, swimmers, and fishermen than any other urb in this book. It's the urban version of popular destinations in the American West like Vail, Jackson Hole, and Aspen, even though it's far east of the Mississippi River. Locals probably wouldn't be shocked to see a kayaker or mountain biker tie up his or her "transportation" at the theater or coffee shop, even though these activities are not commonplace here. For diehard urbanites and outdoor enthusiasts, Northshore is perhaps the best urb of this kind in the country.

Adding to the energy is the bustle on and around the Walnut Street Bridge. This narrow steel trestle linking Northshore to downtown entices residents and visitors to "get up and move!" Completely rehabbed in 1992, the trestle is now America's longest pedestrian bridge, and hosts joggers, walkers, skateboarders, and throngs of regular pedestrians. In addition, rock climbers hang on the rocky trellises. As a result, Northshore is thrilling, alive, and electric. The bridge also links noncar commuters to downtown offices and businesses and hosts truly special festivals one hundred feet above the river.

The Walnut Street Bridge is the link to the Frazier Avenue "see and be seen" promenade. This is the place to get a fresh cup, a newspaper, and breakfast before biking over the bridge to work or grabbing your fishing gear. Although Frazier is only a few blocks long, its bustle acts as a people magnet.

Just off Frazier is one of the south's most unusual and smartly planned urban parks, Coolidge Park. Hosting concerts, joggers and walkers, and impromptu picnics, Coolidge boasts animal statues spitting water on frolicking children; an enclosed 1890s carousel carrying grandmas, children, and lovers; and vibrantly colored sidewalks, all between the river and the refurbished backsides of Frazier Avenue businesses. Here, kids fly kites on the long grassy meadow, and runners gear up to begin a twenty-mile jog at the head of the Tennessee Riverwalk. It's a goose bump–raising urban experience.

Coolidge Park provides a sharp contrast to the urban energy of the nearby row of buildings full of coffee shops, outdoor sports stores, and residential lofts.

The Northshore may well seem like a tourist destination because it combines sports, arts, entertainment, and leisure, but everyday goods and services can be found here as well. There is a local grocery store within walking distance to most areas, and the Walnut Street Bridge allows easy access to downtown restaurants.

The hilly, historic neighborhood of North Chattanooga north of Frazier Avenue is full of bungalows and old Victorians. Infill housing, including urban row homes, is beginning to spring up on still plentiful vacant properties. As the region enjoys a generally low cost of living, those shocked by high-priced San Francisco, Chicago, and New York will find life here to be unbelievably affordable—especially given the unrivaled urban and outdoor amenities.

LITTLE ITALY, SAN DIEGO— "*ITALY*"

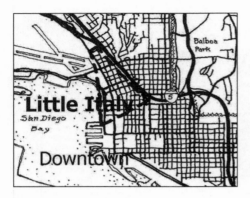

If you've always fantasized about living in Rome, Milan, or Florence, you might move instead to San Diego. The city's Little Italy, the largest of its kind in America, is fifty square blocks, dwarfing lower Manhattan's ten and San Francisco's little Italian strip.

Little Italy lives up to its name in a big way. Italians still inhabit this former tuna and fishing village turned highly attractive and funky neighborhood. It has a semiarid climate (like Italy), Mediterranean vegetation (like Italy), and spectacular ocean views that greatly resemble the Italian coast. Local businesses enhance the theme with Italian surnames on signs, Italian-influenced art, and Neopolitan-style sidewalk ambience. This is a residential dream urb.

This urb is yet another example of a neighborhood devastated by highway construction. The area was split in the early 1970s when Interstate 5 drew automatic, impenetrable boundaries. Most of the land in what used to be northern Little Italy was effectively "annexed" by nearby uptown neighborhoods. Fortunately, the remaining fifty acres just north of downtown San Diego has hypersensitive residents who are determined that the neighborhood's Italian character and charm survive.

Italian character more than survives along Little Italy's premier corridor, India Street, which provides a festive pedestrian atmosphere, especially on the ascent from downtown. Walkers can smell Italy itself emanating from the many Italian restaurants lining the corridor. The sidewalk is alive with lazy strollers, lovers walking hand-in-hand, bikers, and friends enjoying an espresso and cheesecake al fresco while watching the sun set over the Pacific.

During the last decades, India Street has become infinitely more alive with businesses and patrons. Vacancy rates are extremely low,

The low-flying planes roar over India Street, providing an extra level of urban energy and fascination.

and neighborhood services are increasingly prevalent because of the new demand for everyday goods, groceries, and banking services. Someone moving from Iowa to Little Italy might experience sticker shock, but residential opportunities are in reach of many incomes in Southern California.

A continuous flow of cars and pedestrians is welcomed here by the locally famous, perfectly placed, dramatic welcome sign. The twenty-foot art deco masterpiece spans the width of India Street, inviting people up from the downtown valley to "come to Europe." Locals don't want anyone to mistake where he or she is.

An unusual kind of energy also makes India Street special—low-flying jumbo jets. Planes on their way to the nearby San Diego International Airport make their final approach to a major runway directly over Little Italy. The jets rumble and gently vibrate windows, but the peculiarly delightful noise and vibration add much to the urban ambience.

Pedestrians on India Street can almost see the faces of window-seat passengers, who probably wonder about the pretty little enclave below.

Needless to say, demand for Little Italy living is high. Lucky urbanites living in appropriately designed new buildings of varied styles are able to walk to work in nearby downtown, enjoy ocean views, frequent the adjacent "Embarcadero" district, and walk to a nearby light-rail station, making Little Italy too good to be true.

New Little Italians, whether authentically Italian or not, move to the neighborhood to add to the already established theme—Italy. It is clear that the area's character will remain even as throngs of newcomers eagerly arrive.

OHIO CITY, CLEVELAND— "SIDEWALK CULTURE"

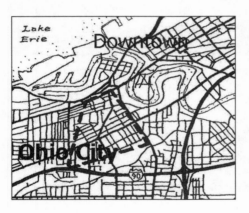

When you think of Ohio, and especially Cleveland, Ohio, "bland," "brown," and "rust" probably come to mind. Those who keep up with cities know that Cleveland is no longer the ugly industrial wasteland of yesterday. Cleveland has received a lot of attention for its downtown renaissance and unique pro sports complexes. Yet, some people still see the Cuyahoga River on fire and smoke belching from factories. Cleveland jokes still persist; the "Mistake by the Lake" just can't quite lose its old image.

Flying in the face of those preconceptions is eclectic, energetic, thriving Ohio City, Cleveland. Far from bland and brown, this urb is full of blues, reds, and greens. For bored suburbanites, a move to Ohio City provides a novel kind of visual stimulation unique in the otherwise content-to-be-beige state of Ohio.

In addition to its color, Ohio City stands out because of its wide variety of cuisine—sit down, take out, "thump and choose," and on the

A typical Ohio City café has colorful awnings, tables and chairs, and lots of people enjoying outdoors.

go—Ohio City is a great place to find food. As in many European cities, people here seem to organize their days around eating. They meet good friends enjoying brunch at little cafés and diners, take power walks after a gourmet meal, and rest under shade trees to "digest." Ohio City is food—good food—and lots of it.

The hundred-foot-tall campanile above the Westside Market can be seen from most of the surrounding neighborhoods, reminding everyone that delicious things are available below. The indoor-outdoor complex is a local icon, beloved, always full of people, and *the* spot for catching up with neighbors on the same food-gathering routine. All kinds of in-season vegetables, seafood shipped same-day fresh, and the gamut of spices and wines are a feast for the senses.

Locals always seem to be carrying food. Telltale brown bags tell passersby you've been to the market, but it's a toss-up whether the contents will last the whole trip home. Impatient pedestrians are often caught wiping fresh fruit juice from their faces. Many others sit in the park chewing warm bread and pastries. Ohio City offers food from the Caribbean, Mexico, France, Italy, Japan, Vietnam, Poland, Germany, and many other countries to tantalize local taste buds. You'd think that everyone would be obese here, but you'd think that about Europe, too. "Eat good, look good, feel good," seems to be the local philosophy.

Ohio City's sidewalk culture is as active as any city's in the world. Chatters and chewers take up most available sidewalk area, and you can't help but feel safe walking around this ultraurban neighborhood. Magnificent skyline views make it feel "big city," and the human street activity makes visitors wonder, "This is Cleveland?"

Sidewalk culture here is also defined by high-energy entertainment. As Cleveland's disco central, Ohio City has a good number of dance clubs, live music venues, and sidewalk nightlife, along with myriad restaurants.

Another intriguing aspect of Ohio City is that people here are a mix of high society and ultracasual "life." Few restaurants have strict dress codes, and some of the best five-course meals are served as comfortably to someone in jeans as to someone in black tie. This place is easy. For those seeking an environment and lifestyle similar to Greenwich Village, Ohio City is perfect. Forget those old notions of Cleveland.

"THE MULTIPLE VILLAGES OF THE"—NORTHEAST QUAD, INDIANAPOLIS

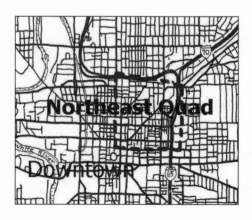

Official downtown Indianapolis is huge. It's so big that several downtowns of other large cities could fit easily inside its boundaries. Two major thoroughfares bisect the area, converging at "The Circle" and creating four "quads." The Northeast Quad provides the most eclectic living experience by far.

This urb is quintessentially eclectic because it offers every kind of urban residence. What makes it even more unusual is that these housing types are clustered within individual minineighborhoods. Within a few blocks' walk of each minineighborhood, the landscape provides an entirely different ambience and attitude. A little bit of everything awaits those who move to the Northeast Quad.

The most intense urban energy is along and near the Massachusetts Avenue Arts District (MAAD for short). This district is a tiny version of Greenwich Village, but shares a similar funky theme. Naturally, MAAD attracts the creative set, gay people, hipsters, artisans, food lovers, and bohemians. Alternative visual and performing arts venues are increasingly moving to the corridor and its surrounding area. The Indianapolis Arts Academy also keeps full-time artists active year-round, and urban nightclubs and coffee shops keep the area humming late into the night. The area offers an increasing number of interesting restaurants, small neighborhood bars, jazz clubs, a bookstore, and a slew of design firms. Although several energy-depleting surface parking lots remain, Mass Avenue's interesting mix of businesses and people is quickly turning it into a full-fledged window shopper's mallternative, full of energy.

MAAD already provides a vibrant urban experience, but its revitalization has just begun. Increasing demand for homes near its urban funk is the reason, and this demand is fueling rapid-fire redevelopment. Rehabilitation of older buildings along the corridor's fairly intact row of business storefronts and newly appreciated late nineteenth-century architecture is well under way.

City lovers seeking a quieter atmosphere, but with easy access to downtown and Massachusetts Avenue's commotion have several great choices. The Lockerbie Square neighborhood, a completely hidden, designated historic district, is immediately east of funky Massachusetts. With a forest of mature trees and quaint single-family cottages, city lovers live here quietly, enjoy the nightlife, and walk home. Although dense and sophisticated, Lockerbie and its sister neighborhood, Chatham Arch, are positioned a lot like a suburb in the middle of the city, with a great downtown skyline view and urban energy just blocks away.

The St. Joseph neighborhood is a stunning historic enclave just north of the arts district. It resembles a dense version of an Indiana farm town, with traditional homes, front porches, quaint landscaping, and wide sidewalks. St. Joseph also adds a splash of the old country with terra cotta formations that embellish many commercial buildings and ancient Tudor-style apartment buildings. Because this area has been so well preserved, its beauty and close proximity to fun, work, and shopping have made it one of the most desirable places in the Northeast Quad urb—and the city—to live.

Row-house enthusiasts will think they died and went to Baltimore. North-south-oriented Alabama Street has brilliantly restored structures alongside new, appropriately designed infill buildings, giving the area a Northeastern coast city feeling. Alabama Street bridges the gap between the ultraurban Massachusetts corridor and the serenity of St. Joseph.

Adding to the mix of housing options are twin thirty-story, high-rise towers. Similar to those found in Vancouver, British Columbia, or Chicago, they fit in with the crazy quilt of residential structures.

The Northeast Quad is as attractive to Manhattan transplants who want a piece of home in Indiana as it is to ex-farmers who are unfamiliar with city life. City living offers a vast array of urban lifestyles. This variety and eclecticism make the Northeast Quad an amazing American urb.

THE FAN DISTRICT, RICHMOND— "LONDON"

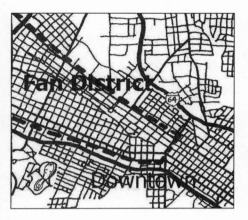

Although it's called The Fan District, this Eclectic Urb is actually a large area just west of downtown Richmond. The Fan (for short) is named for its street grid, which forms a fan shape that extends outward from downtown. Every street is special, from the grand boulevards to the tidy service alleys. This urb is fifty years ahead of its time, regardless of its colonial layout. This is because Richmond apparently had an abundance of city enthusiasts during the sprawling 1950s, '60s, and '70s who stayed around, keeping its antebellum neighborhood alive. The area's preservation and vitality will astound city lovers, most of who have never heard of "The Fan."

Many people captivated by the preserved historic architecture might confuse The Fan with a Garden Urb because of its old-world charm, hundred-year-old trees, and cobblestone streets. The Fan fits squarely in the eclectic category because of its variety of city environments, largely due to the strong influence of artsy Virginia Commonwealth University on its southern edge.

Suburbanites looking to relocate in the city will notice the quality and amount of activity on The Fan's streets first. Although laid out on a city grid, the streets are unpredictable and not easy to navigate. For instance, Monument Avenue, one of the most beautiful streets in the world, is a wide boulevard that catapults cars around circles as pedestrians swirl around the intersections. Drivers must proceed slowly, keeping alert for the dog walkers and other pedestrians in the crosswalk and along the periphery. Alertness is also required because all roads leading off the circles look similar, causing drivers to lose their sense of direction. It's wonderfully unpredictable and aesthetically stimulating. The magnificent streets provide a London-style ambience that automatically attracts Eclectic Urban personalities.

Strawberry Street, so quaint yet so eclectic, offers a wide range of neighborhood services like grocery stores, dry cleaners, delis, and banks. It is a side street, not a major corridor, providing the neighborhood a village center, just like a small town in the city.

In sharp contrast, Broad Street is a wild and crazy four-lane corridor featuring an emerging funky sidewalk scene. Broad Street is the place where skate-punks meet alternative-furniture shoppers, and business professionals converse with bohemians. It also has suburban-style shopping, including grocery stores, mega hardware stores, and fast-food restaurants. Funky urban seems to be fast overshadowing the suburban design, but at least The Fan's residents don't have to travel far for these services.

Then, tucked away in what would normally be just another residential lane, out-of-the-ordinary businesses flourish on Strawberry Street. A quaint village center, Strawberry offers everyday services on a smaller urban scale. Tiny neighborhood grocery stores, delicatessens, dry cleaners, bakeries, coffee shops, cash machines, and fine restaurants line the corridor. Strawberry is especially charming because of its signature awnings of all colors, stripes, and patterns, which hang over almost every building. Still, the mix of businesses and intensely active sidewalks strongly hints of funk.

Architecture is another important asset. The Fan's historic residential architecture is diverse. Some structures are tucked away inconspicuously; others are painted in daring, bold colors. Most look like they were transplanted from England. The most important Fan asset is the attraction it has for urban dwellers in this neighborhood. It's a rare American environment that is home to a complete, authentic, and complex kind of urban lifestyle.

THE ELMWOOD VILLAGE, BUFFALO— *"FOREVER"*

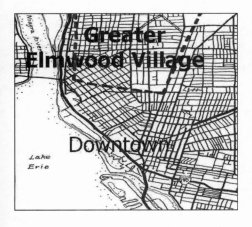

Many people's perception of Buffalo is that it is an ugly, dirty, neglected, shrinking, abandoned, and boring Rust Belt city. Wrong! Buffalo is one of the most beautiful, cleanest American cities with a lot to offer ex-suburbanites and even the most seasoned city people. Anyone doubting Buffalo's ability to dazzle should take a trip down the "Strip"—the Elmwood Strip.

The Elmwood Village is a mile-long elegant Eclectic Urb built around Elmwood Avenue, locally known as the Elmwood Strip. This neighborhood, like many others in inner-city Buffalo, is suddenly hot real estate, after ten years of shrinking property values.

Suddenly, out of nowhere, suburbanites who remain in the region are choosing to move back to the city, and particularly to The Elmwood Village. An incredible range of housing is available within walking distance of the Strip, which has sat depreciating, waiting for decades to be rediscovered. Any residential building, from small fixer-uppers to huge Victorian mansions, garners bidding wars and contracts, sometimes the first day they're on the market.

Elmwood Avenue is one of America's greatest city streets. Can't you just picture yourself liv-ing in this urban neighborhood?

Real estate professionals must be in disbelief. Longtime business own-ers are surely giddy. This is not Las Vegas, Atlanta, or Orange County—it's Buffalo! This city has suffered as much as or more than the majority of American cities in loss of people, businesses, and image. Elmwood is leading the way toward redefining Buffalo's unfortunate (and wrong!) reputation.

Residents here flock to the Avenue to watch people, have dinner or coffee, or shop for antiques. Elderly men play checkers on the same sidewalks where teenagers hang out. Scooter kids join urban rollerbladers, and moms chat while pushing baby strollers. This is sup-posedly abandoned *Buffalo*?

Elmwood is true to its past, with almost every structure built to the sidewalk, abundant storefront windows great for browsing, and a wealth of historic architecture. Perhaps Elmwood works because it has evolved enough to provide everyday people with fast-food burgers and ice-cream cones. This place is refreshingly more than a typical boutique district.

Buffalo's spectacular urban plan is present here. Elmwood Avenue's perfect north-south orientation gets a breathtaking surprise from the diagonal Bidwell Parkway intersection. This crossroad forms intimate triangular miniparks and grassy medians that develop into a broad, simple, yet extravagant commons area. Myriad events and nonevents happen here—farmers' markets, antiques sales, frisbee throwing, jogging, conversing, and picnics. Every square inch of green space is used.

There is something intangible about The Elmwood Village, something good, hopeful, but with a slight imperfection that (ironically) makes it seem almost perfect. Elmwood is a lesson for sterile master-planned communities and will be the catalyst for repopulating the ingeniously planned, captivatingly beautiful, clean, vibrant city of Buffalo. It's no wonder that locals have branded it, "Forever Elmwood." Indeed, this extra-special, high-quality urban environment deserves to last that long.

East Rochester—"Urban Elegance"

As a greater network of interesting neighborhoods, East Rochester is arguably the most elegant urb in the eastern United States. Perhaps this is because it sits immediately across Lake Ontario from the influences of spotless Canada. More likely, it is because of its inspiring street layout. At almost every turn, the pattern changes from ordinary two-way streets, to one-way streets, then to a beautifully landscaped street median, followed by a surprise roundabout. The variation of street widths and orientations is brilliantly planned, ensuring that something special would be constructed here. Elegant is the best way to describe the resulting feeling and energy.

So, too, is the old, historic architecture that could never be built in

The heart of the energetic Monroe Avenue Arts Corridor.

the new suburbs. The variation of styles and the strong building materials are notably permanent and especially colorful. Mature trees, obviously hand planted and perfectly spaced inside the sidewalk medians, hint at the age of the structures in the background. Walking these streets means soaking in a special ambience, including the elegance that sets this urb apart.

A place this elegant doesn't normally evoke images of funkiness. It is the variety that underlies this elegance that places East Rochester squarely in the eclectic category, the combination of assorted neighborhoods that provide an edge to the otherwise graceful surroundings. For instance, The Neighborhood of the Arts (NOA), an area that includes stately academic buildings that were once part of the University of Rochester, is a rare, individual place that is in a perpetual state of planning for visual stimulation. It's a very pedestrian-friendly neighborhood, keeping walkers intrigued by the art they encounter on their local strolls. This area features the "Urban Art Walk," which showcases sculpture, murals, and other visual arts; people can't help but comment, critique, and think. The NOA also features world-class art galleries, an art school, and unrivaled international cuisine. Creativity, which is encouraged, is almost a requisite for people who choose to visit, and especially for those who choose to live in the area.

Other area residential opportunities include quaint cottages on the same street as huge mansions, apartment complexes, and industrial lofts. On almost every street, tree canopies embrace pedestrians, creating a linear social gathering place and a dog walker's dream. To be on any sidewalk in this area is refreshing and empowers the spirit. Adding to the superior urban qualities are small corner shops serving the immediate neighborhoods, making it hard to choose among the wide selection of services and things to do.

The highlight of East Rochester could be the raw energy of East Monroe Avenue and its arts district. East Monroe Avenue is the best place in Rochester for a casual urban stroll, spontaneous conversation, or morning jog. It's also filled with a range of cultural diversity as evidenced by its array of ethnic restaurants. Greek, Indian, Asian, Mexican, and Italian cafés share space with conventional fast-food chains. The theme on Monroe Avenue seems to be complete diversity—some cutting-edge, some regular joes, black, yellow, brown, and white. Starbucks and mom-and-pop cafés coexist. It's about mixing things up, the unexpected, and enjoying the day. East Monroe Avenue is a revered mallternative, partly because it's so down-to-earth and authentic—but so is the rest of the elegant, funky, arty East Rochester urb.

FINDING THE ECLECTIC URB(S) IN *YOUR* CITY

Eclectic Urbs are not as easy to pinpoint as Garden Urbs or Postindustrial Urbs. By definition, they have a mixture of urban architecture, street patterns, and housing types that can vary widely among cities. This loose formula can be effective when looking for any city's Eclectic Urb:

- Determine if the population is eclectic by the mix represented. If there are people with purple and orange goatees, sophisticates, tattooed skin, same-sex partners eating with elderly grandparents, uptight business people, hip hoppers dancing on the sidewalk, or any unusually wonderful mix of people together in close proximity, it's probably an Eclectic Urb.

- If you don't already know where the eclectic side of town is, ask an older store clerk in a suburban mall, young students from a local college, local tourist bureau representatives, and others which area is the "weirdest" in the city. Also count an area as weird if any respondents indicate a place they "can't quite put their finger on." Most cities have at least one such area, and often more than one, that intrigued locals point to.
- A place with the largest concentration of "experimental" kinds of businesses, that is, those that cannot ordinarily be found anywhere else in the city (including restaurants, bars, dance clubs, and book and clothing stores) is likely an Eclectic Urb.
- The most "defining," celebrated neighborhoods (especially in smaller cities) are usually Eclectic Urbs.

The diagram on page 173 symbolizes the varied land uses and structures in a typical Eclectic Urb. Eclectic Urbs often have a smattering of all kinds of urbs, therefore making them a bit more difficult to identify. It is the variety of everything, including people, architecture, building size, and businesses, that makes the urb eclectic.

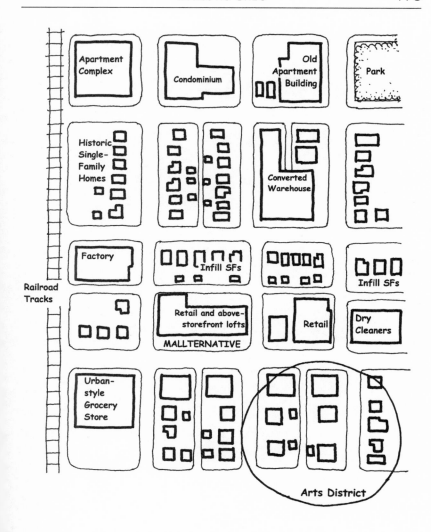

Apartment Complex

Condominium

Old Apartment Building

Park

Historic Single-Family Homes

Converted Warehouse

Factory

Infill SFs

Infill SFs

Railroad Tracks

Retail and above-storefront lofts

MALLTERNATIVE

Retail

Dry Cleaners

Urban-style Grocery Store

Arts District

Are you a funky Eclectic Urbanite? Can you think of any Eclectic Urbs in your city of choice? You might have already pinpointed the Eclectic Urb in your city and are ready to pack your bags. Hold off on your decision; the next category could bring a new perspective to the city you may have never had before.

7

BLANK CANVAS URBS

Every city has a Detroit

You Are a Blank Canvas Urbanite If You . . .

- Enjoy a good challenge.
- Like to know that you are "a part of something happening" and enjoy contributing to positive change.
- Are patient and able to endure years of slow progress.
- Want to make your own mark and be able to influence land use and development changes.
- Are a passionate urban developer who wants to live and develop where the most dramatic differences can be appreciated.
- Do not mind living in the part of the city with the fewest available local neighborhood services.
- Are not scared by empty streets and sidewalks.
- See beauty and hope in boarded-up and abandoned buildings.
- Do not mind living around existing manufacturing and industrial uses.
- Can live in a building not intended for residential living until you arrive.
- Think it would be fun to establish or be a part of a new, active, influential neighborhood group.
- Consider yourself to be an "urban activist."

INTRODUCING A NEW MOVEMENT—URBAN ACTIVISM

Activism has become a life goal for many who contribute what they can, for issues important enough to fight for, to make a positive difference in the world.

Positive change occurs through leaders who are passionate about a cause. Millions of people have adopted their own impassioned cause, an issue important enough to spend money, enthusiasm, and limited time to effect change.

For instance, many cancer survivors offer their services to raise money and visit hospital patients—anything they can do to fight the disease and provide empathy and comfort. Human rights organizations attract minorities and other groups that feel discriminated against to march or lobby for equality and increased representation and opportunity. Some of the most passionate causes are associated with trying to keep something from becoming extinct. Groups ranging from scientists to schoolchildren rally against further environmental degradation, taking a stand against polluters and hoping to stem the greenhouse effect.

The tactics some activists take can be extreme. Tree activists live in trees for months to protest indiscriminate felling to save spotted owls. Groups like Greenpeace, in its little motorboats, confront large fishing vessels. Riots sometimes result from frustration and the need to be heard.

Although many activist groups have made significant gains in such things as saving the whales or raising funds to buy rain forest land that would otherwise be clear-cut, one cause with problems equally as severe has been summarily overlooked. Like the snail darter in danger of extinction by dam building, many American cities are in similar danger. Youngstown, Ohio; Camden, New Jersey; and East St. Louis, Missouri, are notorious for almost ghost-town status. Every American city has vast sections that are in trouble, and some are already extinct. The deplorable quality of urban life in many places should generate the same level of attention as much more popular causes like the rain forest and the ozone layer. This is especially true because city neighborhoods affect American lives more immediately than do dolphins caught in tuna nets. Some of America's cultural bastions, historic places, and sources of original urban energy generators are dying.

This Get Urban! bumper-sticker is the equivalent to "Save the Whales" or "Don't Pollute!" for urban activists who love cities and crave urban energy.

It is amazing that, as all other world causes continue to gain more passionate recruits, America's dead and dying inner cores are ignored or, worse, avoided. What is even more astonishing is that many Americans who love cities and would ordinarily choose an active, fun city lifestyle often dismiss inner cities as lost causes, choosing cul-de-sacs instead. To those people who love cities, choosing to avoid or overlook the state of urban America is equivalent to being a bird lover and ignoring endangerment of bald eagles or penguins being clubbed to death.

There is a movement that hints of urban activism in America. Called by a variety of names, the most popular of which is "smart growth," this cause is fighting urban sprawl or the proliferation of subdivisions and low-density development. These activists are trying to change development patterns, especially on the growing urban fringe (the kinds of places that you want to move from). This movement involves curbing automobile use, encouraging more dense residential and commercial developments that provide mixed land uses that resemble more of a city lifestyle, and preserving open spaces. The problem with this kind of activism is that, while it includes rebuilding cities, it focuses too much on the flawed zoning legislation and design of suburbia, largely ignoring the places that need help the most. There are no comprehensive movements that care exclusively about ailing urban areas. It's time for a new movement—urban activism.

This chapter might be considered the city's version of a late-night infomercial featuring a poor, hungry child from a third world country. These places should tug at the heartstrings of city lovers just as much as those who want to preserve the rain forest or eradicate animal abuse are affected by their causes. Inner cities are where urban visionaries belong, as do people who want to see and be a part of positive change. For obvious reasons, these areas are called Blank Canvas Urbs.

THAT BLANK CANVAS FEELING

Painters view blank canvases as temporary. In their minds, the blank canvases are already painted—all they need are a splash of color, cre-

Broken windows suggest that the buildings have not been maintained, are empty, or have been written off for business tax purposes. The state of an urban neighborhood's windows is one of the telltale signs of its health, hope, and level of urban energy.

Vacant properties that obviously should have many structures built on them are not able to harness urban energy.

Abandoned homes and businesses featuring plywood (the most foreboding building material) deter new residents and are blights on the greater neighborhood.

Although some kinds of graffiti can add to urban ambience, out-of-control graffiti indicates an out-of-control street gang problem, ambivalence, and loss of neighborhood pride.

ativity, inspiration, and compassion. Some look at blank canvases as opportunities to create a potential masterpiece. Similarly, Blank Canvas Urbs are waiting for people, attention, devotion, and even (literally) paint. These places have easily recognizable attributes.

LATENT URBAN ENERGY

In chapter 3's "Getting Urban 101" lesson, Lesson Two taught the importance of understanding urban energy. The level of activity determines a place's vitality, which spawns activities, events, moods, and expressions—all contributing to a city's rhythm and personality. Blank Canvas Urbs, being mostly empty and abandoned, have little activity, scant vitality, few events, bad moods, empty expressions, undetectable rhythm, and strange (perhaps threatening) personalities. Needless to say, the urban energy in Blank Canvas Urbs might be less than what ur-

Surface parking lots eliminate any chance of urban energy. Surface parking lots destroy what could be (or used to be) a continuous row of buildings providing human activity and vitality. Instead, cars sit during the day, and the property remains empty at night. Additionally, a lot of asphalt suggests that the local market considers parking fees more profitable than high-density residences, offices, or businesses. A wasted chance for someplace special in downtown Louisville.

ban enthusiasts are seeking. Lesson Two also demonstrated how buildings, streets, and people interact with the elements that make up urban energy. Where there are few people, remnant or missing buildings, and empty streets, it is hard to imagine why anyone would ever consider living in such a dead place.

Urban optimism is the reason. Some urban neighborhoods have undying hope for and optimism about their futures. As places to live, Blank Canvas Urbs can be the most exciting experiences, because working toward their revitalization becomes a calling, a power greater than oneself. Working for what many people would consider to be a crazy and unattainable goal, urban activists give their time, money, and souls to become part of something that is happening—a magical work in progress.

Any urban neighborhood that has the basic building blocks for success—namely urban street shapes, an intact urban grid, and developable land—has "latent urban energy." Some of the most desolate places in the city can use their urban DNA to plan and build a vital, electric urban neighborhood that could rival or surpass the most successful ones. Blank Canvas Urbs can harness this latent urban energy by building dense structures. They can attract newcomers by building hundreds or thousands of new residential opportunities, creating a new demand where most feared to tread. These urbs can creative new events from scratch, unlike any other in the world, and receive instant notoriety, the kind that makes places special.

The decades of demolition and abandonment that have caused urbs to become blank canvases cannot eradicate the latent urban energy stored on these areas' grids (unless the grids change to curvy streets). In many ways, Blank Canvas Urbs should be the future destinations for city lovers who want to be responsible for building tomorrow's best urban places. Blank Canvas Urbs are exciting because they can be built *from scratch*, they can become anything. Helping such places release their latent urban energy, places that otherwise depict despair and blight, is the goal of urban activism. "Invigorate America's Cities *now!*"

DETROIT—"A GALLERY OF BLANK CANVASES"

As a city, Detroit presents one of America's greatest opportunities for revitalization. But until recently, most people would probably have put it at the top of their list of worst cities. Its image generally has been desperate, burned out, hollow, and depressed. Detroit jokes have risen as Pittsburgh and Cleveland jokes have diminished over the years. Academicians use this city to benchmark their lowest ratings for countless measures, from population loss to urban blight. However, finally there is a new breed of Detroit supporters determined to resurrect their city.

They have a lot to overcome. The city has lost around 500,000 people since 1950 as its suburban region continues to grow and sprawl. It has become the symbol of the "hollow city" surrounded by a vibrant, growing suburban region—the proverbial hole in the doughnut. In other words, those who were able to have fled inner-city Detroit in droves.

Detroit still has some very nice sections, but its many neighborhoods with broken windows, burned interiors, graffiti-covered exteriors, and scary places have become its public face. And because of the mass exodus of residents, sections of Detroit resemble a postwar zone. While skeptics consider the city's crumbling architecture a lost cause, there is an emerging crop of urban enthusiasts who can be convinced that there is still beauty in some of these aging buildings.

Now the question for Detroit's business and government communities is how to attract these urban pioneers to their city. Detroit's reliance on heavy industry, especially manufacturing automobiles, has succumbed to the new information age. Many long-established businesses have abandoned the center city, deepening the doughnut hole as jobs and people followed. Many central Detroit residents must now reverse commute to corporate campuses and service employers in fringe communities. The once powerful factories and strong neighborhoods have been severely hurt by, and remain vulnerable to, this economic change. Social factors, including white flight, poor schools, and crumbling infrastructure continue to sucker punch the ailing city.

City lovers have, until now, considered it a lost cause. One major reason is that most city buffs want to enjoy urban energy and revel in a vibrant and entertaining urban environment *now*. Detroit's terrible reputation as one of the worst cities discourages most from considering a move there. It's time to turn all this around.

The hope and optimism of the early and mid-1900s is back, even though so much of Detroit's urban energy has eroded along with hundreds of demolished structures and empty properties. There is a spirit, a powerful force that is beginning to emerge. The biggest challenge now is to convince the rest of the nation that Detroit and its supporters are working to turn their city around, that local organizations and individuals are working on tomorrow's surprise: *America's best city*.

What if Detroit, against all odds, can emerge triumphant from its negative press and depressed state? What if it can rise from the ashes to become the most exciting and sought-after urban experience? As a city, Detroit resembles a person who has the potential to triumph over adversity. If Detroit can "pull itself up by the bootstraps," it will once again become one of America's most vibrant, wise places, full of character and spirit. Instead of being the poster child for urban blight, it could become the next American Cinderella story.

Cinderella had help from her fairy godmother and mice who could

Not all of Detroit looks like this, but a lot of it does. It is time to look at Detroit in a new way.

sew formalwear. Detroit could benefit from this kind of assistance as well. The city needs thousands of new city enthusiasts who believe in its latent urban energy and hidden potential and are willing to invest in it.

These urban crusaders need to be convinced to look at Detroit in a completely new way. Downtown Detroit has many attributes, especially its urban DNA, to enable it to reverse its fortunes. Its streets are laid out on a superb city plan with a large enough critical mass of squares and rectangles to rival any thriving city. All the city needs is investment, commitment, and most of all, thousands of people who are passionate about the possibility and the idea of cities. For city lovers, there can be no greater cause than to contribute to a vital Detroit.

Pack your bags, roll up your sleeves, and join the cause.

You don't have to move to Michigan to become an urban activist. Every city has a Detroit. America's hundreds of Cinderellas can't make it to the ball alone. The following examples offer some of the best opportunities to be a part of an exciting life adventure—rebuilding American cities, unleashing latent urban energy, and practicing urban activism.

FORT WORTH SOUTH—*"IMAGINE . . . "*

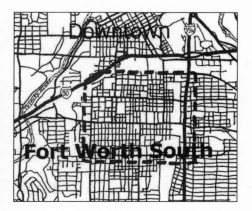

Imagine a place where you can enjoy tree-lined streets, children playing and riding their bikes down the sidewalks, neighbors sipping tea and visiting on their front porches. You stop off at the corner drugstore or the dry cleaners. Or you may patronize one of the new shops at the Village Square. Nearby, exciting research advances in medicine and technology, new businesses spring up and others move into established, rehabilitated buildings. The residential area is safe and attractive with refurbished homes standing next to new traditionally styled architecture. On your way, you wave at the police officer on bike patrol. Landscaped streets come alive with art, antiques, music, and restaurants. A comfortable trolley shuttles passengers between downtown and the vibrant activity along Magnolia Avenue. You arrive home to your Craftsman-style bungalow, surrounded by mature trees and beautiful landscaping. Later that evening, it's time for a night out and you choose dinner at the nearby Italian restaurant followed by a walk down the street to listen to jazz. Sound too good to be true? It's not. (*From Fort Worth South literature*)

Local boosters say that this is what their urb, called Fort Worth South, is all about. It will be, but it isn't yet. Fort Worth South is centered on two large hospitals and a history of neglect. Until a few years ago, this area was called the Medical District, basically a tired place with dilapidated properties, high crime, and not much hope.

The area formally changed its name to Fort Worth South, as evidenced by blue banners with white lettering bearing this new name *everywhere* in the urb, especially on one of its main corridors, South Main Street. This street is still full of boarded-up windows, empty buildings, and very low levels of urban energy. But these banners have

The bold new image of the Fort Worth South Blank Canvas.

changed everything—they have declared to the world that "a new urban village" will be born in this area. The banners represent what urban activist locals insist will happen in their home neighborhood—urban vitality and an urban personality that will attract new residents who otherwise might move to Arlington.

Much more is occurring behind the scenes. Aggressive measures in place to bring unkempt properties up to code are working. The neighborhood is literally cleaning up. Strong business partnerships are growing, and one of America's most inspiring urban activist groups is hard at work making its urb a safe, attractive place to call home. All it takes is a little imagination and hope. Fort Worth South is an exciting Blank Canvas Urb to watch.

FARISH VILLAGE, JACKSON, MISSISSIPPI—
"URBAN SOUTHERN SOUL"

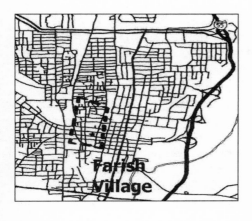

Farish Village is an exciting yet upsetting Blank Canvas Urb—upsetting because of the harsh emptiness of what should be and exciting because of the vision of what could (and should) become a vibrant urban center. This urb has limitless potential and hope that provide a framework to ignite the imagination of optimistic city lovers.

Its character is defined by Farish Street, a north-south corridor about five blocks west of downtown Jackson. This street is almost completely uninhabited, but most of the buildings provide a blank wall (full of latent urban energy) along its entire length. Somehow, Farish Street escaped the urban renewal demolition era, and today it resembles a life-size toy model of abandoned shells.

Farish Street is an urban anthropologist's laboratory for a historically black business district. Old, crusty paint tells visitors that a good-size furniture store once did business here. Evidence of a lost vibrant city neighborhood hides in the remaining walls and sidewalk markings. Freshly nailed "for sale" signs overlap one another. Although plywood has replaced glass on most storefronts, it's clear that this was once an important business corridor.

Immediately surrounding Farish Street on all sides are acres of vacant property, long taken over by weeds and debris. Most of this land has become little-used gravel parking lots. Not many people have the nerve to leave their cars exposed in these daunting places, but, with new buildings constructed here, that might no longer be a consideration.

Farish is a depressing place—for those who loathe cities. For urban activists, it represents an exciting opportunity to shape Jackson's urban future. This is the kind of place about which even those ignorant of city

issues would say, "There should be something here." It's perfectly compact, providing tremendous opportunity for residential density, packed
sidewalks, and vitality, and its buildings seem to demand revitalization.

Someday there could be galleries, museums, shops, dance clubs,
windows for browsing, residential lofts, social service agencies, doctors' offices, bars, drugstores, or neighborhood grocery stores. The few
local restaurants specializing in southern soul food will be able to attract "foodies" from coast to coast. Festivals, parades, and arts sales
could happen here. Perhaps dramatic street events featuring gospel
singing would be appropriate. A monthly "Running of the Armadillos,"
late conversations on the roof on hot Mississippi nights—anything is
possible here. Even in its dilapidated, deserted state, Farish Street offers an exciting opportunity to build a thriving, healthy urban district.
Possibilities here are unlimited, tantalizing, and almost dreamy.

Fortunately, Jackson has designated Farish Street as a local historic
district, thus preserving the structures and paving the way for tomorrow's vibrant urban ambience. Few other abandoned corridors have
this kind of architectural history; preserving them is a great beginning.

There is also a new plan, just in the beginning stages, to turn this
district into a model of Beale Street, the well-known jazz corridor just a
few hours' drive north in Memphis. The kind of activity found along

*Farish Street, a series of old, intact business shells—an exciting opportunity perfect for a
malternative, above-storefront lofts, and urban energy.*

Beale would be an improvement. One hopes that local developers will build a new, exciting neighborhood in addition to a jazz district. Farish Street has too much potential to become just another playground for suburbanites. Something magical is about to happen here.

INSIDE THE INNER DISPERSAL LOOP OF TULSA—*"FUNKLAHOMA"*

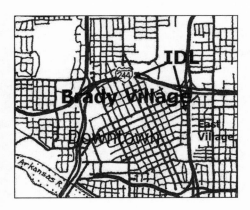

Like so many other cities, Tulsa has a freeway that loops around its downtown. When it was built, entire neighborhoods were destroyed to make way for new overpasses, exit ramps, and asphalt. Locals call this man-made boundary the "IDL," short for Inner Dispersal Loop. Dispersal, in this case, applies more to people, who were dispersed away from the inner city, than it does for traffic.

For such a big city, Tulsa suffers greatly from a lack of urban energy that should be found within the IDL. The downtown, with soaring 1960s-style skyscrapers, is, unfortunately, surrounded by dozens of acres of Oklahoma-size parking lots. In fact, much of the area in and around the IDL is one huge parking lot. But Tulsa's urban DNA, excellent urban grid, and smattering of historic structures could be the city's home for urban activists. New residential buildings holding twenty-five thousand urbanites (even fifty thousand!) could (and should) easily be accommodated here. Today, downtown Tulsa is withering, but it teems with latent urban energy.

At first glance, this area doesn't seem to offer many choices to people seeking an edgy urban environment. A closer look reveals a promising urban future. This is especially true in an area just north of the railroad tracks: from the downtown parking lots and south of the IDL, a Blank Canvas Urb, called "Brady Village." This area has the right ingredients to energize future urban Tulsa.

Brady is an official entertainment district, though not much seems to be happening here. There are a few interesting bars, and the historic Brady Theater is a venue for concerts and plays. Brady also holds a few (interesting) stores, though not nearly enough to be a mallternative. Regardless, die-hard Blank Canvas Urbanites will automatically be drawn here. Its broad streets, intact wide sidewalks, and remaining old structures are waiting for new life.

A city lover's first visit to Brady Village evokes a vision overload. Urbanists' eyes are drawn to Tulsa's magnificent retro skyline, lighting up the southern night sky. The still-active railroad tracks provide an edgy feeling, lots of clackity-clack noise, and old-fashioned grit. Along Brady Street, it's easy to see two dozen five- to ten-story buildings luring thousands of permanent resident urbanites. The first floor of each building could be occupied by restaurants, more bars, a little urban grocery store, laundromat, three or four coffee shops, a local bakery, a public market, and hundreds of tables and chairs lining the entire length of the sidewalks. Although empty today, Brady Village should be the destination for Tulsa's urbanites, despite its current skid row appearance.

Perpendicular to Brady Street is North Boston Avenue, two intact

Surrounded by unsightly surface parking lots and a perimeter chain-link fence, the historic Brady Theater is Tulsa's performing arts venue, hosting concerts, plays, and Broadway shows.

blocks ending at the freeway overpass at the top of a hill. This corridor, although short, is already more urban than Brady Street, with a collection of adjacent historic buildings. Strong potential exists here for sleek, urban lofts, luring the most urban Eastern Oklahomans and others from far away. Condos and urban flats could provide a market for even more sidewalk tables and chairs along Boston Avenue.

Brady Village is Tulsa's logical place for a "funk injection" of dramatic public art and a Brady version of an arch spanning the street's width, or a local icon, perhaps an alternative rendition of a Tulsa cowboy or plains pioneer. North Boston Street could call attention to itself and the rest of Brady Village, attracting urbanites and putting it on the national map of creative places. Local boosters and developers could do all of this. As is the case with other Blank Canvas Urbs, this area's multiple acres of surface parking lots can become its greatest asset. Building on every square inch of these will catapult this urb into a new future, an urban future full of life and energy.

Brady is obviously without a strong theme. All it needs is just a fraction of the number of people who decide to move to suburban Broken Arrow or Jenks to create "Funklahoma"—an appropriate title because Brady needs funk, to be lit up, alive, and pumping with a showy energy, instead of being relegated to its current lifeless, empty shell.

DOWNTOWN HUNTSVILLE, ALABAMA— *"ROCKET CITY"*

Huntsville is Alabama's high-tech hub, nationally famous for having many Ph.D.s and actual rocket scientists. It boasts an international airport, a world-class space museum, a large arts community, and even beautiful Appalachian Mountain views. Yet, with all its assets, Huntsville is Alabama's (and perhaps the entire Southeast region's) biggest suburb without a city.

When NASA's Marshall Space Flight Center was built in the mid-twentieth century, Huntsville was a little town with a little town square. Nearby Decatur, more centrally located in North Alabama, was more of the local "big city." Huntsville was so small that when Interstate 65 was built, the city was bypassed as a link between Birmingham and Nashville.

Then scientists started coming by the thousands, and Huntsville, at least in sheer numbers of people, was fast becoming North Alabama's regional center. The population boom occurred during the age of the suburb. Downtown Huntsville, tiny in scale, must have been considered too small to build up and too insignificant to consider seriously. Besides, modern strip malls and subdivisions were accommodating the population influx.

As a new city, Huntsville needed to prove itself. It constructed what for the time were innovative hybrid freeway systems like Memorial Parkway, a locally celebrated corridor with steep overpasses that tickled driver's tummies like riding a roller coaster. This big road made residents in little Huntsville feel "big city." Then eight-lane commercial corridors were built to replace farm roads. Sophisticated, big-city regional malls, bigger than Birmingham's and Nashville's, padded local egos. A new UFO-shape civic center attracted big-ticket concerts. All the while, most residents didn't need to go to, or even think about, the little downtown square.

As well educated and well paid as Huntsville has marketed itself to be, its downtown is a shame. Even with its tiny scale, urban renewal ripped down the existing buildings, then a new suburban-style bypass was built around the square, and surface parking lots were paved everywhere allowable. A modest duck pond park and a few unimpressive, ten-story mock skyscrapers (including a couple of regional banks and local government buildings) provided a meager skyline, far from a downtown to be proud of. With the resources it used to build suburban roads to access ordinary shopping malls, Huntsville could have been a real city filled with pulsating urban energy. Ironically, its bad planning policy will be its saving grace—opportunity is ripe.

Today's downtown is mostly vacant properties and surface parking lots waiting for urban buildings, sidewalk activity, and thousands of residential units. Fifty years of being the Southeast's largest stand-alone suburb, Huntsville can now morph into a high-quality urban experi-

Some of downtown Huntsville looks like a junkyard. This scene, a hodge-podge of grass, weeds, asphalt, stray rocks, sticks, junk cars, chain-link fences and absolute vacantness is typical.

ence. Just a few significant residential structures could bring about one of the most dramatic, positive changes in any American downtown.

It might be difficult to convince locals that downtown living can be fun. But Huntsville is known as "Rocket City" because of the resident technology and brain power that helped put humans on the moon. That same nickname could help to change the perception of Huntsville as a "noncity," bringing suburbanites who are tucked away in the nearby mountains and river valleys because of the draw of its lifestyle. The city might come up with something fun, kitschy, but historically appropriate. Picture "Rocket Nights," where local crowds and enthusiastic tourists in rocket hats, rocket cars, rocket costumes come together for a Rocket-Gras. Rocket Residential Tower, a building that looks like a rocket, might be the new hip place to live. After all, this is a supposedly modern city with very little historical architecture. Maybe, in the way Phoenix changed its downtown name to Copper Square, downtown Huntsville could become "Rocket Center." Or developers could just build ten thousand housing units and let the locals come up with their own ideas. There's too much potential to do nothing here. A real city is waiting to be born.

Huntsville suffered during the 1990s while the adjacent suburban "city" of Madison became the fastest-growing community in Alabama. With thousands of new people living in the core, this trend could be reversed. Urban activists seeking a true challenge might grab their belongings, then "squat" in the streets, perhaps even chant in protest until a white knight developer can see what they see—an awesome, proud, vibrant, and unique "real" city of tomorrow. Ph.D.s and rocket scientists will surely appreciate the option of local city life.

DOWNTOWN LAS VEGAS—"A REAL CITY"

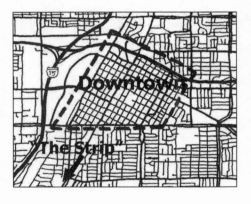

During the last two decades, the Las Vegas area has grown faster than any other in America. Even before this, Las Vegas has long been the world's most popular and famous gambling destination. It is also a big entertainment capital, luring millions to witness everything from acrobats, fire-breathers, and other circuslike productions, to comedy shows, magic extravaganzas, singers, and dancers.

The world sees Las Vegas as a spectacle, a fun place to spend a week in the dry heat. Urban Las Vegas is virtually nonexistent, which is a spectacle in and of itself. Although the city is residentially dense, most of it resembles a huge suburb. Commercial strips, including strip malls and big parking lots, dominate the landscape. The same thing seems to be everywhere, even on side streets: mostly gambling casinos and huge, flashing signs repeat themselves in most sections of the city. The outlying growth areas (like the master-planned "Summerlin" development) are very nice, even dense, but not at all urban.

An unusual irony is the city's world icon, the renowned Las Vegas

Valuable real estate sits vacant, cracking in the sun. Downtown Las Vegas has many such properties, wasting an opportunity to build a vibrant, dense city full of urban energy.

Strip (Las Vegas Boulevard), is not even located in the city of Las Vegas, but suburban Clark County. Even more ironic (astonishing, actually) is that America's fastest-growing city's downtown can be classified a Blank Canvas Urb.

Downtown features the glitzy "Freemont Street Experience," an enclosed pedestrian corridor with the same casinos and tacky shops that can be found a few miles south along The Strip. A new "lifestyle" development is being built adjacent to Freemont, which will likely include similar scenes: more casinos, a few residential units, and other tourist-oriented businesses. Otherwise, downtown Las Vegas resembles downtown Huntsville, Tulsa's Brady Village, and Jackson's Farish Village.

There is good news for downtown Las Vegas, however. It has the setup to lure residents looking for a real city. It's situated on an eastern-style urban grid, and, compared to its immediate surroundings, especially the long suburban-style commercial strips everywhere else, a thriving urban district can emerge here. It has the same assets as all other downtown blank canvases—lots of surface parking lots, a sad little skyline (the original casino hotels), nondescript government buildings, and few real pedestrians. Acres of vacant property can go a long way toward building Manhattan-style density and creating future authentic city vitality.

When downtown Las Vegas offers "regular" city amenities like an arts corridor such as Richmond's Fan District or Milwaukee's Historic Third Ward; twenty-four-hour people as in downtown Charlotte or Memphis; and a stunning urban park like Northshore, Chattanooga, it will attract countless thousands of urban people excited about a move to urban Las Vegas. Because of the area's extraordinary growth, few places have more potential to form an instant urban place. Until then, take a gambling trip to the Fremont Street Experience and roll the dice. Perhaps you'll make enough money to become Las Vegas's first true *urban* developer.

East Village, Des Moines—"High Impact"

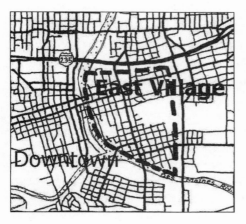

This urb is called East Village because it's just east of the Des Moines River. Though set up to be an urban village, it is worlds away, both geographically and developmentally, from Manhattan's much more famous urb of the same name. When Blank Canvas Urb people discover it, East Village will become the epicenter of quality urban living in Iowa.

It has the right setup— charming Main Street–style corridors, an old-fashioned grid complete with service alleys, and a spectacular view of the surprisingly tall Des Moines skyline. The state capitol's shiny metal dome graces the eastern view. Urban lifestyle seekers will see East Village for what it can become, not what it is today.

Today many important buildings are underused, and some parts of the Village have been obliterated. Buildings have been ripped down, leaving bare parking lots that destroy the neighborhood's continuity. Several structures are boarded up, others sit rotting.

Housing opportunities here are scarce. There are a few small, single-family houses on its east side, some rare storefront loft opportunities exist, and some 1960s-style residential towers flank the northeast boundary. Coming here cold to investigate places to live will probably discourage even the most intrepid urbanite, but the feeling shouldn't last long.

Redevelopment is likely to boom here in the coming years. East Village's perfect geography, constrained by Capitol Hill on the east, the Des Moines River on the west, and a freeway on the north, will force compact development and, eventually, more residential structures to be built here.

It's also bound to happen because this is the home of Des Moines's creative community. An art community is obviously growing, evidenced by huge painted murals proclaiming that art galleries are inviting more artists here. The local gay community's bars add to the landscape, and out-of-the-ordinary ethnic restaurants offer Asian and Mexican cuisine.

East Village is without an apparent theme, and it is also apparent that residents and businesses haven't branded the neighborhood yet. Local

Hints of an emerging Eclectic Urb—a billboard advertising an art festival, pool hangouts, Asian restaurants, and dance bars are dotted among typical blank canvas surface parking lots. East Village is on the cusp of transforming itself into a vital urban place.

boosters might not think of "high impact" as a theme, but they could take lessons from Fort Worth South's "Imagine" to influence this neighborhood reemergence, or choose something similar to The Short North, Columbus's "Art in Your Face" theme—a high-impact statement that would be perfect for East Village.

High impact could describe the elimination of surface parking lots in favor of a critical mass of residents. It would point to urban grocery stores, as locals tell stories of the brownfield they were built on. High-impact streets, brimming with energy, pedestrian activity, and commerce are possible. High impact, as a theme for East Village, is proactive, prophetic, and fitting for such a visually and functionally perfect urban space.

Longtime East Villagers might want to take a photo inventory. In the next five to ten years, this urb could be filled with would-be suburbanites who want authentic, big-city living in Des Moines. With a little effort, East Village can become one of the most energetic, Eclectic Urbs within hundreds of miles. Empty properties can transform into neighborhood businesses, storefronts can have happy renters upstairs, and parking lots can become affordable apartments and luxury condominiums. When this happens, East Village could justifiably be a "high-impact" urb.

SoLo, Kansas City— "Fill-in-the-Blanks"

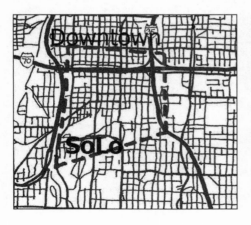

SoLo, named for its location just south of downtown Kansas City's inner freeway loop, is a blank canvas Postindustrial Urb that will intrigue urban activists. Today it is a mostly empty, dusty, forgotten place, one that most people would hurry through. First-time visitors' "fill-in-the-blank mechanism" will be stimulated by the half-filled (or half-demolished) nature of development. Some corridors feature dazzling warehouse buildings with intact early twentieth-century architecture, others are flanked by scarcely used surface parking lots.

You can just imagine people everywhere—on the balconies of new loft buildings and in the windows of old ones, on the sidewalks, in the new outdoor cafés, and inside apartments where people live and work. It is so intriguing, so tantalizingly raw, that even without a building frenzy occurring (yet), SoLo will set the imaginative city lover's mind soaring.

No apparent development is happening here, but it should be. SoLo evokes the same feeling as visiting an embryonic Strip District, Pittsburgh, Historic Third Ward, Milwaukee, or SoHo itself. It is the rust, the industrial hard-edged materials, and the realness of the place that are so wonderful, even in the area's currently pitiful condition.

The majority of Kansas Citians think of SoLo as a "nonplace." Locals probably consider it to be "just another empty part of downtown," oblivious to the name "SoLo" and any superior urban qualities or potential. But plans are in the works for a full-on urban transformation here, and the name "SoLo" is part of the plan.

A master development is in the initial planning stages for this area, using the design of LoDo, Denver (lower downtown), as a model. The

SoLo is poised to become a quality Postindustrial Urb. Its streets already have a "cold canyon" effect that is attractive to urbanites.

city has realized the power of SoLo's unbeatable urban location and almost infinite development possibilities. The master plan proposes a few "big-ticket" development anchors such as a stadium, a movie theater, and intricately designed public spaces. Fortunately, the SoLo plan concentrates heavily on residential development.

If implemented, SoLo will fill a niche for people wanting a city environment that cannot be found in Kansas City's current urban offerings. SoLo will also appeal to locals who do not want to live in "too perfect" places. It will provide Kansas City with excellent skyline views and funky, spontaneous street life, and it will fill a gap between the city's two major employment centers—downtown and the Crown Plaza area just south.

Whether or not the master plan is implemented, there are subtle hints that SoLo is beginning a quiet revolution. An old warehouse in the middle of the urb sports a sign that reads, "SoHo South Lofts," as this converted warehouse is south of the "SoHo Loft" rehab in downtown Kansas City's Garment District. Small infill successes, including habitation of older commercial buildings, are happening behind the scenes. An upstart arts community is gathering south and west of the SoLo boundary, where housing is currently more available.

This urb won't stay a blank canvas state for much longer. It might also put urban Kansas City on the world map.

MIDTOWN, BIRMINGHAM— "MAGIC"

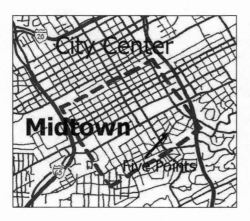

Even though Birmingham is the largest city in Alabama, hard-core city lovers will find it hard to fill their needs there. Overall, urban energy is lower than low. The few people walking on the sidewalks probably have no choice. Funky residential opportunities are scarce, other than a few loft conversions in the struggling downtown.

Birmingham generally fails the city lover looking for a true urban lifestyle.

This mid-size city in the sunny South looks more like 1970s Cleveland than it does Atlanta or Nashville. The nickname, "Pittsburgh of the South," refers to its heavy steel industry history. Its scraped urban landscape is the result of a postindustrial economy that cleared acres of what used to offer thousands of blue-collar factory jobs.

The Vulcan, a statue representing the god of steel, overlooks Birmingham from Red Mountain. He can see hundreds of square acres of urban removal and blight on the north side. If he could turn his head southward, he would see the sprawling suburbs, filled with families trying to avoid this vast wasteland just to the north.

As Pittsburgh has cleaned up its image, revitalizing its core and redeveloping the surrounding inner-city neighborhoods, much of Birmingham remains ravaged. Dozens of city blocks have been leveled and replaced by surface parking lots or weeds. It's a great place for Blank Canvas Urb types to dream, with abundant infill growth opportunities—especially in the roughly one-square-mile area just south of the Center City, sometimes called "the southside," but referred to here as "Midtown."Midtown contains acres of surface parking lots, underused low-rise industrial strips, and a vast, empty feeling. Still, city lovers should be able to recognize that a latent momentum is building, with energy centered on the only real sign of life—the "Five Points District."

Five Points, where five arteries converge, provides a faint hint of what a high-quality urban experience can offer. It's the place for city lovers to do "city" things, like mingling with sidewalk strollers, sipping coffee, reading at the outdoor café, admiring public art and elegant fountains, and watching the traffic and sightseers. Southern soul food, nouvelle fusion cuisine, and jazz swirl together. Everyday staples are available here, too. This place is obviously special, beloved. The rest of Midtown is absolutely devastated, resembling Detroit—Midtown is, after all, a Blank Canvas Urb.

Midtown's potential is limitless. Unlike most other empty urbs, it is home to one of the largest college campuses in the state and a major local employer, the University of Alabama, Birmingham. Around fifteen thousand students spend time here every day, with hundreds in dorms and a few in off-campus apartments. The campus also has a nationally

Five Points, a circle created by the junction of five city streets, is an island of urban splendor in a sea of urban blight and abandonment.

renowned research hospital full of professional, smart, creative, and often well-paid people.

As an economic development tool, the mostly commuter campus has not contributed much to creating a special place. Most students and hospital personnel leave quickly when class and work are done. But UAB and daring infill developers can combine to create urban vitality and energy.

Between wide pockets of blight, Midtown is gaining a few new art galleries to entice creative minds that see what most metro residents cannot. A few have begun occupying scaled-down lofts, making do with few daily survival services. Like Fort Worth South (see page 185), this is the place to build an urban village from scratch. Midtown could easily house thousands of new residential lofts, revitalize the canyons of abandoned structures, and create Alabama's most lively and sought-after urban experience.

Midtown already has planted "seeds" to expand its successful eclectic, lively Five Points intersection. It could take full advantage of the university and hospital to lure new creative minds. Dreamers and visionaries should consider pioneering in Midtown, an incredible urban success waiting to be realized. When this happens, Birmingham will live up to its old nickname, "The Magic City."

KING-LINCOLN, COLUMBUS, OHIO— *"AFRICAN-AMERICAN HERITAGE"*

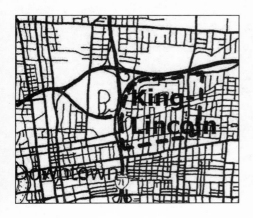

Long Street, just east of downtown Columbus, Ohio, was Black Columbus. Especially during the first half of the twentieth century, Long Street business thrived by serving the majority of Central Ohio's black community. To Columbus, this area was just as important as Harlem was to New York—the epicenter of thriving businesses and cultural heritage.

Today East Long Street has some of the highest concentrations of vacant properties in Columbus. The stores, restaurants, blues and jazz clubs, and apartment buildings are all gone, leaving behind gravel, dirt, and asphalt.

Fortunately, one of the most important structures, The Lincoln Theater, still stands. Intact but crumbling until recently, the theater is being restored to its original splendor. It hosted jazz greats of the past and rivaled Beale Street, Bourbon Street, Chicago, and St. Louis as a thriving cultural arts district. Today, the boarded-up building is a reminder that the segregated (but thriving) African-American community of yesteryear existed. Tomorrow, a special new urb will emerge.

The newly dubbed "King-Lincoln District" is poised for rebirth. The black community has been inspired by Columbus's successful inner urbs, wondering why this couldn't happen on Long Street. It will. Several African-American developers who love Long Street's past are making the dream come true for near northeast side residents.

"King-Lincoln" is named for the historic Lincoln Theater and the Martin Luther King Arts Complex, a short walk north. Ironically, this area will

The Lincoln Theater, currently abandoned and awaiting its imminent rehabilitation.

become vital again because of the urban renewal that killed it forty years ago. The vacant property is very buildable, with intact infrastructure and a blank canvas for outstanding architecture and urban storefronts. Dozens of properties that have been vacant for decades because of neglect and simple disinterest are now available.

Surrounding the empty land are very old, mostly dilapidated, single-family structures in need of overhaul. These neighborhoods are historically significant, extremely attractive, and lined with mature trees. With a kick-start along Long Street, rising property values, paint, and new wood, there's no reason why this section of inner-city Columbus couldn't thrive like many other, similar neighborhoods.

Local government and greater community have created a neighborhood plan involving many local stakeholders and residents. Their visions are to create a thriving business and entertainment corridor on Long Street and a haven for culture, especially for Afrocentric artists.

If you're a blank canvas type, and you appreciate African-American culture, you may well want to consider moving to King-Lincoln.

THE COMBINED URBS OF CINCINNATI

Cincinnati has many urbs in all categories, but because of its special social circumstances, all of these urbs, regardless of their category, are included together here as an entire blank canvas city. Physically, this city
shouldn't be on a blank canvas list. Most of its neighborhoods are
structurally intact and architecturally dramatic. Its stunning downtown
provides a big city pedestrian experience and incredible vistas of the
surrounding hills and the Ohio River. Cincinnati is one of the most
beautiful cities in America, comparable to older Eastern cities like
Boston and Philadelphia, and even some in Europe. How, then, could
the entire city of Cincinnati fit into the blank canvas category? Simple,
its reputation.

Cincinnati has endured as much negative national press in the last
fifteen years as any of the most notorious cities. From an incident that
happened more than a decade ago, its entire population is still pigeon-
holed as a puritanical bunch that made an international spectacle of
themselves about controversial art in a local museum. It is known as
being historically intolerant of gay people and the site of tremendous
racial strife and out-of-control race riots. Unlike other industry-heavy
Rust Belt cities, Cincinnati never quite modified its Rust Belt image to
postindustrial "SoHo cool." As a result, its young people have been
fleeing at alarming rates, and because of its widely publicized reputation for uncompromising conservative nature, most young hipsters
would never consider moving there to start their careers.

The absence of superior neighborhoods is not a problem in Cincinnati; however, population loss is. Since its prominence as one of America's largest and most important cities during the industrial age of the
early and mid-twentieth century, Cincinnati has lost nearly half of its
population, which threatens to dip below the 300,000 mark, hardly a
major city today. But things are changing.

Cincinnati has begun an aggressive campaign to turn its image
around. Locals who love this city are some of the most forward-thinking,
organized, and enthusiastic urban activists in America. They range from
young people to CEOs of multinational corporations. Turning the city
around has become part of the culture. Cincinnati residents know they

have to do something positive, and do it quickly, to bring new people and new life back to the city before it's too late.

Blank canvas types who are looking to make a positive change should consider Cincinnati seriously for many reasons. Because the riots were a terrible blow to the local image and economy, and because neighbors were rioting against neighbors, the city is confronting the painful subject of race relations head-on, an issue most other cities refuse to face. Many individuals, and even influential Procter and Gamble, are pushing to repeal an infamous city ordinance that allows discrimination against gay people to prevent losing or failing to attract the lucrative "creative class." Developers are taking risks in providing new downtown housing and refurbishing empty buildings in the beautiful but beleaguered Over the Rhine neighborhood. Obviously, a lot of work is being done in Cincinnati to welcome all kinds of new city dwellers.

City lovers and passionate urban activists should contemplate a move to Cincinnati because of its inspiring new take-charge spirit. Cincinnati has grabbed the national spotlight in news stories featuring cities on the rebound. Locals want to make it so tantalizing and irresistible, that no one would ever choose the suburbs. But, with the

city's status as a blank canvas city with a negative reputation, change might be more difficult than in a lot of other cities. Building houses on empty properties and dead downtowns is comparably easy. In Cincinnati's case, once its reputation is improved, it will rival, and then surpass, the urban lifestyle offerings of the "cool" cities.

This blank canvas is an incredibly beautiful place. It's a mid-size city with a big-city ambience. Its infrastructure was built for a population more than twice its size, and it's preparing to welcome throngs of new enthusiastic city lovers. What are you waiting for?

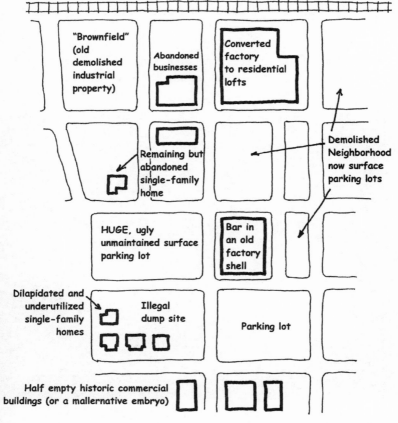

This diagram symbolizes the emptiness and potential that exist in the typical Blank Canvas Urb.

FINDING THE BLANK CANVAS URB(S) IN *YOUR* CITY

Blank Canvas Urbs are easy to find—they're the obviously ravaged urban places. Depending on their original layout and functions, they can become Postindustrial, Eclectic, or Garden Urbs and can be found in any section of the center city. The formula for finding the Blank Canvas Urb in your city is easy:

- Find the most embarrassing areas of the city that you think could become an urban showplace.
- Look for seas of parking lots.
- Notice the boarded-up or abandoned houses, commercial buildings, and properties.
- Seek the areas with the most litter and the fewest people.
- When your mind starts seeing what the place could be instead of what it is, you're likely to be in a Blank Canvas Urb.

If you are a Blank Canvas Urbanite—or any urbanite, become an urban activist.

8

CONSIDERATIONS FOR FUTURE URBanites

So, which urb will it be—SoHo, Savannah, Greenwich Village, or Detroit? From what you've learned in chapter 2, you should understand the method for identifying quality urban places and the various kinds of city environments to match each personality. You should also be able to pinpoint specific geographic locations to land in an authentic city (from chapter 3). This chapter builds on this base and offers other important considerations to ponder and tools to prepare before your actual search begins.

FIND YOUR URBAN LIFESTYLE (101)

Pick the city you want to move to and buy a foldout street map (found at gas stations, convenience stores, and bookstores). The map should be detailed enough to identify the different suburban and urban street shapes. Open the map on a table, grab a highlighting pen, and use it to find the area of the city that is truly the city. Remember from chapter 3 to consider the following key lessons learned:

Identify the REAL City Limit

Outline or highlight the area of the map that contains rigid shapes, including squares, rectangles, triangles, and perfect circles with protruding straight lines (if applicable). Try to pinpoint the line of demarcation between the city and the suburbs and disregard any reference to a city limit boundary on the map. With your marker, clearly write, "The REAL City Limit," on the map (try not to mark over the squares and circles). Draw an arrow to this part of the city to indicate that it's the primary focus of your home search.

Avoid Streets with Suburban Shapes

On the squiggly line side of your drawn real city limit line, put in big bold letters: **THESE STREETS WILL NOT PROVIDE AN AUTHENTICALLY URBAN LIFESTYLE.**

Identify the Downtown

The next step is to find the city center. If there's any reference to a city hall building, a state capitol (if applicable), or areas central to the rest of the squares and shapes, it's probably the downtown. If the city is unfamiliar, search the Internet for "Downtown City X" and try to find landmarks or even the exact boundaries of the city's downtown. When you find it, label it, because this is where you should begin your search for an urban lifestyle.

Try to Identify Urbs

You might not be familiar with a city's downtown neighborhoods, but the maps will help by indicating their DNA. Try to conceptualize what kinds of neighborhoods might exist around the downtown. See if there are any areas defined by a certain shape of street. Try to find place-names on the map that may give hints about what might be there. Again, the Internet is a good source of information. You might find neighborhood sites using a search engine and the proper key words.

Estimate Distances from Downtown

Generally speaking, and using a larger city as an example, two miles is a good benchmark to use as the *outermost* limit for your search—even if urban shapes continue farther out from the city. This depends on the size of the city. For guidance use a two-mile radius from the center for

500,000 or more people in the city proper (populations are easy to find out—check the back of a road atlas or the Internet); one mile from the center for 250,000 to 500,000, three-quarters of a mile for 100,000 to 250,000, and a half-mile for under 100,000. Keep in mind, although they can work well, these numbers should only be used as guides— every city is different. The point here is that, without getting too hung up on numbers and population, you should train yourself to think of living as close to the downtown as possible. Your map's mileage calibra-tion line should be able to help you determine the distance that should be your maximum limit.

Your map should be ready to take to the streets. But don't go until you brush up on what urban quality means and, specifically, what it means to you.

HONE YOUR URBAN QUALITY CHECKLIST

Chapter 2 featured the items that should be on an Urban Quality Checklist. These items are intentionally general guidelines that encour-age users to add their own urban qualifiers. Using this list and adding additional personalized features is a foolproof method for finding an urb as individual as you are.

Begin by choosing a city to move to and planning an urban field trip. This may mean taking a short drive down the freeway or flying across the country. Actually walking the streets, talking to potential neigh-bors, and feeling what kinds of possibilities an urb can offer are the only ways to be sure what kind of life that particular place will offer.

Doing the preliminary research presented in chapter 2 is crucial. The only way to do this research is by visiting the neighborhoods to ex-plore the urban grid in person. Along with your marked-up city street map, take several photocopied pages of the Urban Quality Checklist (a blank one is provided below). Take enough copies so that you can eval-uate the urbs you plan to visit. Don't skimp on details when writing about what you see and the images and feelings you experience.

Doing thorough research enables you to contemplate options and compare and contrast different urbs. Remember to add any extra cate-gories that are not offered on the list and analyze how each urb matches your specific needs, personality, and lifestyle. Take photos of important places and scenes and attach them to the corresponding checklist. If you're not sure which urb to choose, or it's a close call, looking at the photos and reliving the experience through your responses on the checklist will make the decision easier.

Because many people spend more time picking out the right car or clothing than where they live, it's important to actually use the Urban Quality Checklist. Also included is a bonus section that asks how you would describe the urb's personality and energy, as learned in chapter 3. These questions allow you to explain your findings and let your gut talk. They will help match an urb's place with your personality.

URBAN QUALITY CHECKLIST

Date of Visit:

Urb Name: _____ **(URB)** _____ **(CITY)**

Quick Directions: _____

_____

Urb Type (circle one): Postindustrial   Garden   Eclectic

Blank Canvas

Neighborhood and Districts: _____

_____

_____

Check the following that apply:

1. Is it in a close-in urban location? Yes ___   No ___

How far is it from the downtown? ___ **blocks** ___ **miles**

2. Are there a variety of services and land uses? Yes ___   No ___

What kinds are most appealing or those that you would use regularly?

_____

_____

_____

---

3. Is there at least one mallternative? Yes ___   No ___

Where? What street(s)? _____

_____

What is there? _____

_____

4. Are the streets and sidewalks active? Yes ___   No ___

How active? _____

_____

5. Can you tell if this Urb is growing or dying? Growing ___
Dying ___

Evidence: _____

_____

6. Does this Urb provide transportation choices?
Yes ___   No ___

What kinds? _____

_____

7. Does this Urb have a great urban park? Yes ___   No ___

What is its name? _____   Where is it? _____

How and when would you use it? _____

8. Is a wide diversity of people evident here? Yes ___   No ___

Explain: _____

_____

9. Does it seem like a creative place? Yes ___   No ___

How do you know? _____

_____

10. Does this Urb have "urban optimism?" Yes ___   No ___

What did you detect? _____

_____

_____

BONUS SECTION:

Describe this Urb's energy and personality (including activity, vitality, events, moods, and rhythm):

_____

_____

_____

Is this place congruent with your personality? Is this place *you*? Explain.

_____

_____

_____

(STAPLE PHOTOS, MEMENTOS, AND OTHER REMINDERS TO EACH CHECKLIST COPY TO REMIND YOURSELF OF YOUR EXPERIENCE HERE.)

POSITIONING YOURSELF

Selecting the most beneficial location for your new life is crucial in your search for "home." The best way to illustrate the concept featured in chapter 2, called "positioning yourself," is by using a fictitious example. Meet "Jennifer."

Jennifer considers herself to be an "eclectic" kind of urbanite. She recently accepted a job in a distant city. During the interview visit, Jennifer fell in love with what she defined as an eclectic urban neighborhood. A review of the Urban Quality Checklist confirmed that "South Granston" matched her personality in every way—diverse architecture, "weird" people, creative activities, and lots of art. It was also not far away from where she works. Jennifer identified the urb that she wanted to live in and began the process of finding exactly where in the urb she will look for a home. Jennifer began the process of "positioning herself."

Here is some basic information about Jennifer:

- She is fifty-four years old and single.
- She just got a job in the downtown area, about a mile away.

- She is considered middle income, making a slightly below average salary for the region.
- Jennifer is an avid painter, jogger, dog lover, and movie buff and loves to meet new people and make interesting friends.

The first step for Jennifer is to find the services that are important to her. Since she is a painter, she was immediately attracted to the South Granston Street corridor, a thriving mallternative. There are several places there for her to buy art supplies and a number of frame shops. Just south of the mallternative is a doggie daycare/veterinarian's office that even has a pet food bakery. Jennifer has already met nice people there who even asked if she'd like to join them for morning dog walks.

A movie theater is about four blocks north of the mallternative, and Jennifer knows she'd be a regular there. She's also picked out a coffee shop she thinks will be an excellent place to meet people as evidenced by the varied age group that always sits outside on the sidewalk (including many middle-aged people). There are two parks, one larger one near the mallternative and a smaller, pocket-size park on the northeast side.

Jennifer is selling her suburban ranch house and wants to buy a new place in the city. She knows her new home will likely be much smaller than her ranch house because of the attractiveness of the area and higher costs. She would like an entire room devoted to painting and understands that she'll have to stretch her middle-income salary to afford a place like this.

Jennifer compromised with a small 850-square-foot condominium that has a good-size bedroom that can double as a studio. Her building is steps away from a movie theater that shows art flicks, a few blocks from the mallternative and art stores, two blocks from the pocket park (where she often paints), and two blocks from the big park where she jogs daily.

She traded her SUV for a subcompact car that she hardly uses. Lower car payments and insurance premiums were more than enough to justify the city move. She rides the bus to work and only has to walk out the front door of her building to catch it. When she returns home on weekdays, she has established a routine of shopping when she gets off the bus, then walking a few blocks home with bags full of food for dinner. The aspect of South Granston that she is most excited about is the diversity and varied ages of people with interests similar to hers. Jennifer now thrives in South Granston. She is glad she did her urb homework because her personal research and visualization of what life would be like in this neighborhood were right on. Jennifer positioned herself correctly.

New city dwellers must position themselves like Jennifer did. When beginning the research to find an urb, write out specific hobbies, activities, and kinds of events you need to experience every day. There is a blank form, called "Positioning Yourself," below. Use it to direct your search and after you've found your urb by filling out the Urban Quality Checklist form. After completing these two steps, where you will be happiest will be clearer.

POSITIONING YOURSELF FORM

If you've found an urb that suits your personality and lifestyle needs, make sure you'll have easy access to the things that will enhance your city life.

Urb Name: _____ City: _____

1. **Roughly sketch the major streets and landmarks in the square provided.**
2. **Name your five favorite activities and hobbies:**
3. **Locate areas in the urb where you can participate in these activities.**
4. **Locate your workplace** (if it's not within the urb, use an arrow to point in its direction and estimate the distance in numbers of blocks or miles).
5. **Locate the bus stops.**
6. **Locate places where you'll find everyday food (grocery stores, public markets, etc.).**
7. **Locate the mallternative.**
8. **Locate parks.**
9. **Locate any other important places you plan to frequent.**
10. **Estimate the exact location of the middle of your new world. Draw a big, bold star there. Try to position yourself as close to that star as possible.**

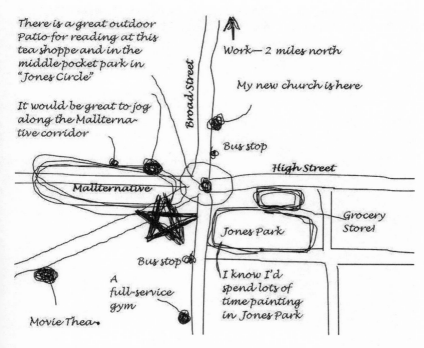

A sample sketch of the "positioning yourself" process with potential "home" location marked with a star set where favorite activities are located.

The most innovative cities are beginning to organize "expos" to help newcomers position themselves; these events can provide a more enlightened and comprehensive approach to a wider variety of neighborhoods. Expos are also beneficial because you can explore urban opportunities as part of a group and in a more organized way. The "city living, dc style!" Expo is an excellent example (see below); it asks participants to "find the neighborhood that suits your lifestyle" and discusses the benefits of local city living. Look for this kind of expo to be held in cities everywhere in the coming years.

The "city living dc style!" campaign is part of Mayor Williams's effort to bring 100,000 new residents into the city. The campaign is a partnership between the office of the deputy mayor for Planning and Economic Development and the Washington, D.C. Marketing Center.

ACCEPT THE URBAN-SUBURBAN COST-OF-LIVING TRADE-OFF

Buying or renting a place in an urb could be prohibitive or surprisingly reasonable. Depending on which city and particular urb you target and your personal income, the cost of living will vary considerably.

Urbs in San Francisco, New York, Chicago, Boston, and many other well-known, long-established, and attractive big cities rank high in urban quality. American city lovers dream of living in these cities, and, as a result, they have high housing demand and low supplies. Hundreds of lesser-known cities that have never been in the national spotlight have *much* lower costs of living. In addition, heartland urbs have urban environments that are just as exciting as those in San Francisco and New York.

Generally speaking, suburbanites who are used to big cheap houses with huge yards often consider the cost of living, even in midland cities, to be extreme. A two thousand-square-foot, single-family home with a grassy, half-acre lot in the suburbs will likely cost less than the same-size home with a tiny lot in an attractive urb. Life in the city is a cost-benefit trade-off.

In popular, "hot" cities, homes can be two, three, or even ten times the suburban price. Heartland cities (those not considered popular or "hot") offer much cheaper home prices, often cheaper than in their suburbs. In most cities, however, homes usually offer smaller (often much smaller) living spaces and yard sizes for the same price of new homes in new subdivisions. A lot of suburbanites don't understand this and have a hard time coming to terms with this difference.

The reason for this discrepancy is a combination of simple economics and lifestyle factors. For instance, tract homes in the suburbs are built on relatively cheap cornfields and meadows. Huge tracts of land (sometimes a hundred acres or more) are purchased together. A typical subdivision developer offers buyers a limited number of house models from which to choose, which lowers development costs because the materials used are exactly the same, and they are offered by the same vendor. Construction supplies are bought in bulk and matched to exacting specifications house by house. Big developers also offer their own financing, often with lower mortgage rates than those offered by banks.

It's a different world in the city. Housing prices and rents depend on urban quality and popularity. For instance, beautiful older homes in well-maintained historic districts are naturally in high demand and are priced as such. Crumbling homes in desperate need of rehabilitation are also priced higher if the neighborhood is perceived to be "up and coming." And, of course, a vacant structure adjacent to a crack house can be bought for a song. As anywhere else, location, location, location applies in the city—no one wants to live next to a crack house.

Urban residential development opportunities are found on small properties instead of wide-open suburban cornfields. Single pieces of developable urban land can have more than one owner (each of whom wants top dollar) and might need treatment to eliminate any environmental contaminants (which is very expensive). Development is usually more difficult and costly in cities.

Other factors that drive up city prices are surface parking lots. In desirable neighborhoods, these are eyed for residential development even as they continue to generate substantial parking fee income for their owners. Naturally, these parking lot owners insist on getting top dollar for their often strategically located parcels of land.

It's clear that, compared to the suburbs, urban areas' scarce land availability and higher land costs are bigger challenges to home buyers and renters. Higher city land costs are only part of the cost differential. Urban life is becoming desirable, and more people want to live in or near the middle of the city. New businesses and fun places are popping up, sparking interest and demand. People are paying higher prices for smaller city homes with no yards, gladly trading their large suburban tract homes and big yards for a unique city lifestyle. The benefit of having a quality city to live in means living "small."

Instead of grass, urbanites are paying for an entire neighborhood. Short walks to destinations where residents can play, shop, relax, work, and spend time are considered to be worth the small, relatively expensive living space. For many city dwellers the exhilaration of city life far exceeds having the pleasure of having grass and patios. This explains why a tiny efficiency apartment in midtown Manhattan costs as much as a mansion in the suburbs. The combination of a close-in location and an unrivaled quality of life doesn't come cheap, but most people can afford it if they accept a smaller-scale lifestyle.

People with low incomes won't be able to buy a spacious loft apartment in Manhattan (or a mansion in the suburbs). Regardless of income, most anyone can afford to live in a quality city neighborhood—just expect tight quarters.

Homes surrounded by great urban places are often much less spacious than those in an ordinary subdivision. For instance, in posh urbs, low-income earners may only be able to afford around 500 to 750 square feet of living space, while higher-income residents might live in a 2,500-square-foot home. Middle-income residents fall somewhere in between. City spaces are much smaller than the expected 1,500- to 4,000-square-foot tract homes in today's new subdivisions. Small spaces and tight squeezes are the norm, regardless of how high the rent or mortgage is. It is the city, after all.

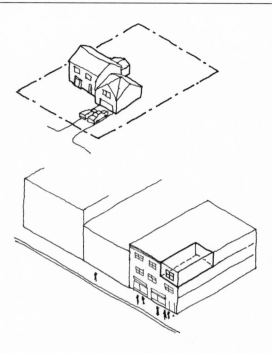

Fortunately, many redeveloping cities want to attract and keep people with a diversity of incomes. They have begun working to ensure that a good mix of home sizes is available. While it may be late for San Francisco and other popular cities, most heartland cities have time to plan. Regardless, city living represents a cost/space trade-off.

If space is important, and so is living in an urb with high urban quality, expect to get less and pay more than most similar-size homes in the suburbs. If the space/cost factor is too much to bear, there are plenty of new subdivisions with model houses available. If you want an urban lifestyle, you might have to get rid of extraneous possessions; try mini-storage or double up. For urban enthusiasts, the benefits of being comparatively cramped will probably outweigh the costs.

FIND AN "IN-TOWN" REALTOR

If you're planning to purchase a home in an urb, one of the most important first steps is finding an "in-town" Realtor. The easiest way to find out if a Realtor is "in town" is by where their listings are located. A general Realtor's listings are spread out over the city and suburbs (even farms). Suburban Realtors concentrate their efforts in the suburbs (thus the name), selling houses on golf courses and in tucked-away cul-de-sacs.

In-town Realtors' listings are mostly in their "adopted" urbs, places they're passionate about. Some specialize in older structures that need work. Many will know each home's history, including the people and their family stories. They will also be aware of the general maintenance and structural issues of old buildings because they probably have sold the same one several times. In-town Realtors have the experience to know the particulars, including quality contractors and do-it-yourself hints for a needed rehab job. A lot of in-town Realtors have been through a rehab experience and have become experts in this field.

A big benefit is that in-town Realtors know the "urb" lingo. Immediately after telling one that you're looking for a "urban garden lifestyle," he or she knows it means a garden, an abundance of mature trees, and his-

Park bench advertisement for Village Real Community in Nashville, Tennessee.

toric residential architecture—and will know exactly the places to show first. The same goes for postindustrial lofts or a funky eclectic neighborhood. General and suburban Realtors might say they know, but they won't have nearly the geographic knowledge and personal insight that an in-town specialist can provide.

Asking for the Realtor's written mission statement is also an effective way of knowing whether he or she is officially "in town."

Urban Living, Houston, Texas: "Welcome to the #1 source for downtown & urban living in Houston! Urban Living 2000 is the place to find New York–style lofts, restored historical buildings, upscale townhomes, modern condos, and other real estate in the downtown and surrounding areas of Houston. If you crave something eclectic, out of the ordinary, & convenience to all the restaurants, nightlife, museums, arts, and offices that downtown has to offer, urban living is for you! Suburbia it's not—cool it is."

Dooley and Company, Columbus, Ohio: "Though one-third of their business is in outlying communities, Dooley and Company REALTORS® tends to focus primarily on the downtown, revitalized neighborhoods of Columbus. Not straying far from his roots in the business, Bruce maintains an ongoing interest in the rehabilitation, not only of historic homes, but also of the neighborhoods that sustain them."

Monroe Properties, Richmond, Virginia: "Simply put, we are real estate developers. But, if your mind turns to subdivisions, malls, and golf courses, you have us all wrong. We turn our backs on suburban sprawl and celebrate the pleasures of urban living. We specialize in the renovation of historic and architecturally significant buildings, with styles ranging from the antebellum to the art deco. We believe in preserving the craftsmanship of the past while installing completely modern systems in our buildings, resulting in a perfect balance of comfort and character."

BUY AN URBAN HAVEN

There are significant differences in buying a city house or condominium versus one in a typical suburban subdivision. The most obvious is greater variety. Architectural styles, interior space, size of urban gardens, distance from the front of the structure to the street vary widely. So do the ages of the structures. Because of the available choices, searching for a house in an urban neighborhood can be exhilarating. As when choosing an urb, this decision should match your preferences regarding cost, level of maintenance required, and, especially, architecture.

Many people who are drawn to the city are attracted to "period" architecture in historic residential neighborhoods. Historic homes are some of the most sought-after structures because they are well built with substantial materials. Each tells a story of the people who lived there, contributing in many ways to the home's appearance. They are also the most intricately preserved structures, retaining the fine construction details that existed when they were first built. Depending on the area of the country and the distance from the downtown, historic homes can be seventy-five to two hundred years old or more.

Urbanites also seek out older neighborhoods full of homes that need work. While many structures in these areas only require cosmetic work, such as new siding or windows, just as many need major reconstruction. Many such neighborhoods can have dozens (even hundreds) of homes that are in obvious states of disrepair, some abandoned or boarded up.

This doesn't keep people from falling in love with these structures (or neighborhoods), especially considering their relatively cheap price tags. Often these houses seem affordable, but their asking price may not reflect how much new owners will have to put into them to make them habitable. Fortunately, many urbanites see dilapidation as a potential finished masterpiece; their vision is compelling enough for them to undertake the tremendous home repair challenges ahead. (They also hope the rehab project won't become a money pit!)

Many factors must be considered before buying an old home, foremost of which is evaluating your own level of home repair skills, available time, and patience. Even more important is determining the home's specific rehabilitation needs. Hire a professionally certified home inspector, especially one who specializes in old and historic residential structures. The inspector will point out what needs to be fixed, any interior and exterior code violations, and help to determine how much money is needed to make them habitable. (Never put an offer on an old house without a professional inspector's report!)

Another consideration is that houses in transition might not meet the local building code standards and might have dust and harmful odors, leaky windows and roofs, and other undesirable or unsafe living conditions. You may need to live elsewhere during the renovation, so the cost of rent, a new mortgage, and rehabilitation funds should be considered as well. You should also factor in the cost of a good security system if tools and construction equipment are left behind at night. For many people, the accomplishment and pride associated with a fixer-upper is worth the headaches and costs that accompany this process.

City living today does not necessary mean buying an old fixer-upper, however. A new residential construction boom is going on in almost every city. The term, "new build" (also called "in-fill" houses), had been reserved for suburban meadows and cornfields turned subdivision. Not anymore. Many urbanites are enjoying the same kinds of low-maintenance living that accompany new construction. New builds attract people who don't want the hassle or cost of rehabilitating older homes.

Moving into a new build means that appliances are still under war-

Major reconstruction on a historic single-family home.

New row houses, Society Hill, Philadelphia.

ranty, structural wear and tear has yet to begin, and building materials are tight, which translates into lower utility bills. People who don't have the time, patience, or skills to do home repairs or major construction have made new builds a hot commodity.

Such construction varies in price depending on size, area of the country, and an urb's desirability. New builds are often more expensive than older structures. Considering the time, sweat, and trouble associated with rehabilitating old homes, new builds can end up being worth the extra cost. In the long run, new construction may actually be less expensive than unpredictable rehabilitation.

New builds take many forms. Single-family homes fill gaps on residential streets, row homes frame the sidewalk in higher-density areas, and mid- to high-rise condominiums are built on old surface parking lots.

Imagine: subdivisions no longer have a monopoly on new. New builds make this an exciting time to buy a home in the city.

RENT A LIFESTYLE

Renting an apartment, loft, townhouse, or single-family home offers several advantages for suburbanites auditioning their chosen urb. The greatest advantage is for people who can't afford to buy a new home. Renting allows them to determine whether they want to make a long-term investment in a particular area. Even if they are correctly positioned in an urb, circumstances may prohibit new city dwellers from buying. Deciding to sign a six-month or yearlong contract provides an escape if a particular urb turns out to be a bad fit.

Rental units are always built in high-profile locations in the middle of already established or emerging urban activity. Apartment buildings are usually built around exciting urban developments to stimulate business activity and provide a critical mass of residents. In almost every city, rental opportunities are found in the very middle of the ur-

It is easy to spot "high profile" urban rental opportunities like this one in downtown Louisville. One singular apartment complex is bringing new momentum and sparking urban energy.

ban energy, above attractions, alongside entertainment, and steps away from fun.

If you're planning to rent, remember to be positioned accordingly. Search rental opportunities in the area, visit property offices, tour available spaces, and try to imagine living there. You're likely to find just the rental opportunity to begin an exciting urban life. In addition to quality locations, another obvious plus of renting is that it's often cheaper than buying. In the majority of heartland urbs affordable rents are probably easy to find. Some of the most desirable and vibrant urbs also offer reasonable rents (along with small apartments), including industrial lofts, above-storefront flats, and apartment complexes. People with limited funds might choose a pay-by-the-week rooming house or find one or more roommates to share rent and utilities.

Renting also means avoiding maintenance responsibilities, which frees up time and eliminates out-of-pocket expenses. Calling the landlord when something breaks is a luxury homeowners don't have. This is why renting makes sense for people with busy lifestyles.

UNDERSTAND CITY TRANSPORTATION

Cars are suburbanites' link to the world and all good things in it. If a suburbanite wants a soft drink, he or she has to drive to a convenience store. Satisfying a craving for a double cheeseburger and large fries means a trip to a drive-through window. Groceries, postage stamps, wine, a loaf of bread, a cup of coffee, a drink at the local bar—anything and everything usually requires a car trip. Suburbanites love cars and why not? They can be one of the most dependable, reliable things in their lives (if they're well maintained).

City dwellers often need cars, too. Many of today's jobs are in far-flung suburbs that are usually unreachable by public transportation. Most department stores are in new suburban malls. People doing home repairs or rehabilitation work require many trips to do-it-yourself mega hardware stores, which are almost always located in the suburbs.

Cars are important for medical emergencies and other unexpected trips as well. They're good for getting away from the hubbub and going to the country for day trips. Many urbanites love their cars as much as suburbanites love theirs, and they're relatively easy to store in the city (on the street, in a garage, or in a driveway).

To a hard-core city dweller, not having a car (or at least not using it very much) is ideal. In most urbs it's easy to buy everyday goods without driving anywhere. Living close to lots of businesses and services is one of the primary reasons people move to the city in the first place. Not having or relying on a car for everything is the best training for city life.

Training to be carless might not be easy, and being in close proximity to everyday services can be hard to get used to. Easy access actually presents a strange irony for freshly transformed suburbanites—walkable city services can be too convenient.

Living in the city and walking to buy that cup of coffee or loaf of bread sounds great—if new city dwellers can actually bring themselves to do it. The ten-minute walk to the movie theater is easier and less expensive than driving, sitting in traffic, paying for parking, then walking to the theater. Like a horse from the old pioneer days, suburbanites have relied on their beloved, dependable car to take them from point A to point B. If point B is only steps away, new city residents are forced to rethink their lifetime relationship with their cars.

Suburbanites and cars are like smokers and cigarettes—it doesn't make sense to smoke, but some people do so anyway. This relationship is also mental, similar to breaking up with a lover. Using a car for everything is not a habit that's easily broken. The relationship can also be compared to growing up and leaving the nest. Adults still love their parents, but they don't need them as much as they did when they were helpless children. Being smartly positioned in a quality city location automatically makes the human–car relationship less important.

Soon after moving to a full-service urb, many ex-suburbanites find themselves mentally conditioned by decades of repetition, much like Pavlov's dog. Unlock. Get in. Crank engine. Back up. Drive forward. Stop. Get out. Lock. Repeat. It's astonishing how many times most people have done this during their lifetimes. The ingrained habit of being inside your beloved, dependable, comfortable, private, and convenient car will require reconditioning. You'll have to learn to walk instead, at least to get things.

Part of that conditioning is rationalization. For instance, walking two blocks for bread is a fraction of the distance people normally walk across huge parking lots and the maze of a suburban mega mall. That two-mile power walk on the mulch trail loop around the golf course seems logical. The idea of walking on urban sidewalks for goods and services might seem like a foreign, almost crazy idea. Thinking about it rationally demonstrates how sensible the idea of keeping the car parked really is.

Reconciling the lack of parking spaces in the city is extremely difficult, too. Spaces are expensive and hard to come by—a popular topic of complaint. City dwellers should think twice about complaining about the lack of parking. Chapter 3 demonstrated how surface parking lots kill urban energy and make it impossible for neighborhoods to harness that energy. When parking places are scarce (which often means that spaces are not available directly in front of a destination's doorstep), this usually means that businesses are surrounded by a vital, sought-after urban environment.

Coming to terms with the fact that parking is simply unavailable is another big challenge to new city dwellers. The way to meet this challenge is to stop complaining about the lack of parking spaces and find other ways to get around.

Learning How to Walk Again

As a suburbanite, you've probably never really considered walking to be a viable mode of transportation. You probably haven't walked anywhere important since the day you got your driver's license. Or you may never have walked to a store or to work in your entire life. *It is at that moment when you discover how to walk functionally that you truly begin authentic urban living.* Being outside of a car makes it possible to detect subtle nuances that cannot penetrate all that metal. Sights, sounds, smells, and the rhythm that makes local urban neighborhoods special becomes very apparent. When you walk, you also begin to learn about and understand your neighborhood.

There is something extraordinary about carrying just-purchased goods home. You'll feel like a European (or at least "big city") walking home with a fresh loaf of bread and eating it immediately. Walking for a double dose of "wake up" mixes the day's weather and caffeine. Besides the exercise, you're using human energy instead of foreign oil for functional trips. Being able to walk to many convenient places is also a testament to successful positioning.

So is the ability to move from place to place via public transportation. Your first time on a bus or train will demonstrate the sensibility of mass transit. A chauffeur (or driver) worries about the traffic, which allows passengers to worry about nothing. In addition to the uniquely urban sensation that comes with having multiple options for movement, being able to choose many ways to move around means personal freedom.

It also means personal expression. Just as choosing the make, model, and color of a car reflects an individual's personality, so does deciding to use a bicycle or a motorized scooter, colorful rollerblades, edgy skateboard, moped, bicycle, or Segway. All of these are viable options for shopping trips, going to entertainment venues or a friend's house, or commuting to work. Moving around the neighborhood in your own individual style is a simple and fulfilling pleasure. Many others who have chosen their own expression of movement add neighborhood interest and street electricity. This aspect of a suburban to urban relocation is often one of the most thrilling and fun.

Urbanites will probably remain on good terms with their cars. Breaking off the love affair gently opens up a world of new and possibly more fulfilling transportation relationships.

MASTER THE ART OF "SCHLEPPING"

In suburbia truck beds, backseats, trunks of cars, and rear sections of minivans and SUVs are normally used to transport goods. Dumping personal belongings here is easy and requires little thought. Suburbanites can pack whatever items they may need when traveling from home to work and back again.

It's different in the city. Quality urban life involves a lot of walking, biking, and using public transit, which makes transporting goods much more of a challenge. Keeping things dry, intact, and light enough to carry comfortably requires thought and organization.

Schlepping is a term many New Yorkers use to describe carrying things. It is a science that urbanites must master, and the best way to do this is to have the right equipment.

Canvas tote bags are good for daily grocery shopping. Fill them up yourself at checkout and throw your groceries over your back on the walk home. "Paper or plastic" will never be needed again.

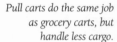

Pull carts do the same job as grocery carts, but handle less cargo.

The equivalent to backpacks for hikers, pouches for cyclists, and trunks for suburbanites, "schlep bags" become an extension of the urbanite's body. Schlep bags are good for holding daily items such as lunch, wallets, cell phones, briefcases, bug repellent, sunscreen, workout clothes, water, snacks, change for transit fare, purses, and any other everyday items that need to be toted. From the moment suburbanites arrive in the city (just like car trunks), these bags become one of their most functional and used possessions.

There are many different kinds of schlep bags as there are city

Urbanites use their arms efficiently to carry especially important items. Fragile goods or fresh dry cleaning cannot be stuffed in the schlep bag or thrown in a cart.

dwellers. The best are easy to carry, water- and weatherproof, and have enough compartments for efficient and functional urban journeys. Their design, color, and material should also fit each owner's style and personality.

The most effective schlep bags have shoulder or back straps that should be strong enough to swing moderate weights from shoulder to shoulder or from shoulder to back. Good ones have zippered compartments that allow easy access to personal items. Some have double zippers that meet in the middle so that bags can be secured with a lock. Hooks outside the bag allow the most serious schleppers to attach or tie on extra items when the bag's interior is full.

You can buy bags in boutique stores that are made for sophisticated schlepping, but you probably already own a bag that can help you schlep. For instance, nylon and polyester gym bags are excellent schlep bags. Shoulder straps are long and strong, zipper components secure multiple items, and interior sections are large, and the synthetic material

Schlepping will eventually become another normal part of your daily routine.

expands for stuffing. Ordinary school backpacks also work for shorter trips when schlepping fewer or lighter items. Carrying weight on your back enables you to walk farther and faster.

Shopping in the city, especially for groceries might be hard to get used to because it means having to haul the groceries home. This is especially true for people with no good excuses for not schlepping—those who live near local grocery stores or city markets.

The best teachers for hauling groceries are the local "grocery cart people" who stroll their carts down the street. These people are functional and brilliant thinkers—finding a way to haul a lot of "stuff" easily as they walk. Unless they have overfilled their carts, they can maneuver curbs, potholes, and even hills. You can learn much from these clever people. (Grocery stores often sell older carts cheaply.)

There are many more ways to schlep efficiently. Before moving to the city, think about the best equipment for carrying things on a daily basis. There is no correct way, only your way. Just like transportation freedom of choice, creative schlepping is an expression of individual taste and personality. In this way, although schlepping looks like work, the act can be one of the most rewarding parts of the day. Have fun schlepping!

PREPARE FOR URBAN CONDITIONS

Suburbanites are accustomed to living inside cars and buildings, with only brief periods of exposure to outdoor conditions. It will take you some time to get used to urban weather conditions. Being involved in a fun, new city life means spending time on the streets and sidewalks, regardless of the weather.

The environment of the city can differ considerably from that of the suburbs. This is part of the intrigue of urban living. It's ironic that, in this way, urban life has more in common with the open range than the sprawling suburbs—people have stronger ties to the weather because it affects their daily routine more significantly and directly. Here are some simple, but important tips to prepare for city weather.

Heat and Sun

The hard, dark surfaces of the city absorb heat and sunlight more readily. Urban heat islands can be as much as ten degrees warmer than the outlying countryside. Prepare for the heat by dressing appropriately, packing bottled water in your schlep bag, and even carrying ice in a thermos. Urbanites spending time on the hot streets must be careful to keep hydrated and have access to fans or air conditioners as well. The bottom line—cities are hotter than suburbs.

Cold

For people living in cold climates, winter is the season when they'll use their schlep bags most. They can be stuffed full of winter-survival necessities, such as gloves, hats, weatherproof overcoats, instant-heat bags, hot coffee in a thermos, scarves, earmuffs, and perhaps a change of socks. Especially when you're walking or waiting for the bus or train, your face, hands, and extremities should be covered.

Winters in cold cities are also times for appreciating a great city location. Few weather events ever paralyze your ability to move because most of the world is just a walk away. Just grab your schlep bag and try to keep warm and dry.

Wind

Dense cities create urban wind tunnels, channeling wind through man-made canyons. The wind accelerates in blustery gusts, often catching pedestrians off guard, and urbanites can become prone to chafed and dry skin, chapped lips, and bad hair days. Prepare for windy weather with lotion, lip balm, and easy-to-fix hairstyles on blustery days.

Urban Glare

Glass-and-metal buildings, hot refractive pavement, and bright sun can be hard on your eyes. Urbanites should invest in a heavy-duty pair of sunglasses with lenses that absorb the sun's ultraviolet rays. With as much time as you'll spend outdoors, good sunglasses will become an important and necessary possession.

Selecting an Umbrella

Picking out an umbrella that is durable enough to withstand being blown inside out (which often happens in urban wind canyons) is important. An urban umbrella should also be retractable so it can fit into a schlep bag.

Coping with Urban Environmental Irritants

Man-made elements caused by industry, transportation, and construction create daily challenges, especially to pedestrians. Automobile and bus emissions can be irritating, and on windy days, flying debris— those little particles slightly larger than dust but light enough to find eyes—often do. Each city and urb has its own set of irritants, so be ready to deal with them.

Urban environmental conditions are not exceptionally brutal, but they may catch new residents off guard. Being outdoors and outside of climate-controlled automobiles means dealing with local weather elements as a part of daily living. Urban weather events make city life even more exciting. Most urbanites would rather be closer to the elements than spend hours inside a car. No wonder new city dwellers are often called "urban pioneers."

UNDERSTAND—AND TAKE CHARGE OF— YOUR FEAR OF URBAN CRIME

Most suburbanites fail to understand that, as places to live, many city neighborhoods are as safe as the suburbs. Sleepy-looking communities aren't always safer places. According to FBI crime statistics released in 2001, a great many small towns and suburbs have comparable, and sometimes much higher, crime rates than do big cities. For instance, in 2001, Gretna, Louisiana (a New Orleans suburb), had a murder rate that is 64 percent higher than New York City's and 38 percent higher than Los Angeles'. Terrell, Texas, a Dallas/Fort Worth suburb, reported more violent crime than Fort Worth and only slightly less than Dallas. Even the remote town of Bend, Oregon, reported a 32 percent higher murder rate than the state's largest city, Portland. In fact, the vast majority of small towns and suburbs have crime rates that are often not significantly different from those in cities. A simple Web search can reveal many eye-opening crime comparisons such as these.

Residents of Gretna, Bend, and Terrell probably consider their towns to be safe, and, in their defense, they are. The key point is that small towns, farms, or even gated subdivisions are not completely cut off from the greater world. Take the Columbine, Colorado, high school shootings in 1998; the suburban Washington Beltway Sniper murders in 2002; and the Elizabeth Smart kidnapping in suburban Salt Lake City, as a few well-known recent examples. The size of a place usually means an increase in the *number* of criminal acts (more people means more actual crimes), but it doesn't necessarily mean that you'll be a sitting duck just because you live in the city. In fact, the odds that you'll never experience a crime as an urban resident are probably about the same as those for people who live in a smaller municipality.

Still, nothing else makes suburbanites as skittish as city crime. Moving into a neighborhood with *any* level of crime is usually why people are reluctant to consider life in the city. The threat of being a victim should be kept in proper perspective—you probably won't be. Like a person who is afraid to fly and ends up becoming a pilot, many suburbanites who would never go to the city because of crime can end up loving the urban lifestyle—and then moving there.

Once they arrive, suburban transplants usually find that full-time urban life isn't scary at all. In fact, the city has a lot more nice people than mean ones, and most people don't succumb to paranoia.

Indeed, some cities and their urbs do have serious crime problems, and new city residents need to become aware of their surroundings. They begin to know their neighborhoods well enough to interpret what's normal, what's suspect, and when illegal activity may be occurring. Many neighborhoods work hard to make them safer. New residents can become empowered by banding together with local crime watches and security alliances dedicated to "taking back the streets" from criminals.

Since September 11, 2001, American cities face a new threat—terrorism. Like all other crime, terrorism can happen in a suburban shopping mall just as easily as it can in a downtown skyscraper. Fortunately, the likelihood that city dwellers will be involved in a terrorist attack is minuscule. That already overused saying, "Don't let the terrorists win," is especially poignant for urbanites, causing many of them to become even more committed to city life.

For many, living in the city means having faith in humanity and hope for the future. After all, the measure of a city's size is how many people live there. Urbanites choose to be city types because they want to experience the full human condition—even if it's flawed.

The overwhelming majority of city dwellers are law-abiding citizens, not criminals or terrorists. Many suburbanites who want to live an urban lifestyle first have to come to terms with the real and perceived threat of crime, and whether (usually misguided) fear will prevent them from doing what they want to do. Statistically, you're much more likely to be hurt while driving on a suburban street or a freeway than you are while walking down most city streets.

In the final analysis, new city dwellers should be aware of their surroundings, trust their instincts, and be realistic about the threat of crime.

They should concentrate on enjoying the benefits and positive qualities of their new city homes.

BLEND INTO YOUR NEW NEIGHBORHOOD

Middle-class and wealthy people—whether white, black, yellow, or brown—who are moving to the city, may be accused of contributing to *gentrification*. Anyone unaware of the word gentrification, won't be for long after settling in a new city environment. Gentrification literally means, "The middle class moving into a poor neighborhood." The word has taken a life of its own. Usually it's interpreted to mean displacing, or forcing out, poor people who can no longer afford to pay their rising property taxes or rent. As a result, these less-well-off individuals are forced to leave the neighborhood. This displacement is the result of a sudden increase in surrounding land values, apartments turning into condominiums, or rising rents, which make it impossible for low-income residents to stay. All of these events can happen because the neighborhood and greater urb has become more desirable—as they should.

Both the word and the phenomenon of "gentrification" generally are used in a negative way by many observers of the urban scene. When an urban area considers gentrification to be mostly negative, existing residents are on guard, wary of new and different neighbors. Having this kind of barrier to city neighborhood population growth, however, is a distinct threat to increasing urban energy. Without waves of new people, cities die. As a new city resident, you can and should, by your motives and actions, work hard to help to change how gentrification is viewed.

This is important for many reasons. During most of the twentieth century, middle and upper economic classes fled inner cities in droves to populate the suburbs, leaving behind the poorest of the poor. Disinvestment set in, and formerly nice neighborhoods became ghettos. As a result, many cities died slow, painful deaths. In the sixty-year period beginning about 1945, many center-city neighborhoods lost between 20 percent and 75 percent of their population. With the loss of residents, these urban neighborhoods lost much of their residential tax base; they lost vital public services such as police and fire protection;

the quality of schools eroded; and once-thriving businesses left empty shells almost too numerous to count. This mass out-migration almost killed most American cities.

A mass in-migration, of course, can harm cities as well if done improperly. The remaining writhing neighborhoods and their current residents don't need a double-dose of devastation—they need to be invigorated, inspired, and filled with new energy. *Everyone* should be allowed to share in the excitement and hope that new people, new businesses, and increased interest bring to rediscovered inner-city neighborhoods.

Indeed, many urban neighborhoods work hard to lure people back to the city, rather than watching as new suburbs extend ever farther into the countryside. Several urbs (for example, the "New Urban Village" of Fort Worth South and Buffalo's "Forever" Elmwood) have branded and themed their image to attract new investors, businesses, and residents. The majority of urbs want suburbanites (as well as country folk, other urbanites, and anyone else) to think enough of their area to spend their days, nights, and money there.

Some neighborhoods use the word gentrification as a war cry. This is especially true if they don't like the people who are moving in. These groups are usually labeled—they may be "yuppies" (young urban professionals), gays, bohemians, or people of a particular race or culture. More than any other, "yuppies" and gentrification seem to go hand in hand. The word yuppies, along with its original meaning, has come to be defined by many locals as "buzzards that swirl over houses and other properties seeking to live an exclusionary lifestyle at the expense of the greater existing neighborhood." New residents (especially those accustomed to years of suburban sterility) often are eager to clean up the area. The established residents, however, feel their neighborhood is being invaded, rather than being cleaned up. Everything becomes "changed," and change can be and often is threatening and disruptive to old-timers. This is especially true if new residents exude an air of snobbishness.

Gentrification is associated most often with the most popular cities because of the high demand to live in them and their scarce housing opportunities. Nowhere has this been more publicized than in San Francisco during the 1990s when the "dot-comers" invaded many neighborhoods, particularly the Mission area. There, the charm, spontaneity, and "funk" local residents enjoyed seemed to change almost overnight. Many

San Franciscans were extremely unhappy about the yuppie invasion. Locals were concerned over a phenomenon, called "monoculturalism." In other words, the yuppies got rid of funky. Cheaper residences for artisans, people with low incomes, and a wide variety of "weirdos" who contributed to the district's unique charm became scarce. Then, the dotcom boom busted, and the techies went broke. But it was too late. Many San Francisco neighborhoods already had changed beyond "repair." A lot of people considered their once weird and wonderful urbs to be little more than bland, expensive, vanilla enclaves with suburban mind-sets. They blamed this on what many would describe as a tragic invasion of the inner city by people who "belonged" in suburbia.

Lower-income people who live in city neighborhoods have seen gentrification happen or are fearful that it will. Even in totally devastated neighborhoods, some locals don't want the middle class (and especially rich people) to "invade" their inner-city areas. They fear the changes to their own lifestyles that newcomers will bring. They are also reluctant to see a dramatic rise in property values, or inexpensive apartments turn into condominiums, thereby displacing low-income renters and eliminating diversity and eclecticism. Some of these people are justifiably fearful and angry.

The great majority of American cities that are not on either coast, or are otherwise "hot" cities, have areas that house very few inhabitants to displace. Such areas include brownfields—vacant properties and dilapidated structures—that have destroyed urban energy and have contributed to the rotten core of many cities. Residents and leaders of hundreds of neighborhoods that have been suffering from dangerous streets, economic despair, and social blight wish something positive would occur. A concentration of poverty and despair, one might argue convincingly, can be much more destructive than a gentrified San Francisco. In places such as Tulsa, Des Moines, Huntsville, Detroit, and the majority of American cities without the allure of Boston, San Francisco, or New York, a middle-class return is the *only* thing that will save them. Either they attract and grow new people, and especially those who ordinarily live in suburban communities, or they wither and die. Most cities have become tired of dying.

Even with the knowledge that central cities have lost huge numbers of people, the gentrification debate continues. But it's hard to believe that people in such cities as Cleveland, Buffalo, and St. Louis (and countless others) could claim convincingly that their cities are being harmed by gentrification when they have lost thousands of residents to the suburbs. *Cities have no chance to survive without continuous waves of people moving in.*

Fortunately, as a result of the incredible central city abandonment, Detroit, Buffalo, and St. Louis, along with most other American inner cities, have vast land areas where little of value exists. Many of these plots of land (brownfields) could hold one, ten, twenty-five *thousand* people. Without filling in their devastated "holes," cities have little hope of ever growing and prospering. People who are excited and willing to move to the urban core are needed for this to happen.

For established neighborhoods, new city dwellers have an important responsibility. They must view their move as an act of compassion, rather than as one of hostility. They must integrate into their new neighborhoods and create positive change, rather than grabbing land and staking claims. Suburbanites turned urbanites also must be aware that established neighbors may consider their habits, tastes, hobbies, attitudes, and worldviews to be alien and threatening. The key is to integrate responsibly. Specifically, this means not expecting the rest of the neighborhood to look, act, and feel like a suburban cul-de-sac.

Responsible urban integration (a positive phrase that should replace the negative, pessimistic, and toxic "gentrification") means volunteering in local community groups, actively contributing to the health of neighbors (new and old), and becoming part of how the neighborhood defined itself before you came. It means thinking twice about contributing to anything that threatens existing families, including buying buildings that might displace people from their homes. It means becoming a part of the community, not railing against it. It means reaching out, finding friends, and helping to make a better neighborhood. It means becoming a positive part of the community. In most cities, there's still plenty of room for growth.

As a new city dweller, you can and should take action yourself. Attend city council meetings. Add to the existing funk in your own way. Meet the people on your block. Support low-income housing plans, especially if they blend into the greater neighborhood. Look out for and value your neighbors. Remember from chapter 2, the more diversity in a city neighborhood, the more energy it is likely to supply. Regardless of your skin color, ethnicity, religious background, financial status, or other "difference," *you should anticipate becoming a healthy part of that diversity*.

A few cities that are experiencing extraordinary displacement have enacted local rent controls, time restraints, and other rules governing transition of apartments to condominiums and mandating availability of smaller units for lower-income people. Many local governments consider it their responsibility to create opportunities for everyone to be able to live in the city. Most heartland urbs are years away from experiencing any effects of real gentrification. Therefore, plenty of time remains for them to plan preemptive measures and address income diversity. In the meantime, middle- (even high-) income people should not feel that moving to the city is immoral or "bad." People should move to the city for a quality city lifestyle and because they love urban places, just as they would move to a golf course community, a beachfront, a trailer park, or anywhere else. Simply understand the responsibility that accompanies such a move.

Understand also that, as a new city dweller, you shouldn't accept responsibility for causing harm to an urban neighborhood that has been in decline for decades. Instead, be thankful that you have an opportunity to become a contributing member of a reemerging neighborhood. Your move is better for society, the environment, and urban places than if you hid away in a bland and exclusionary suburb. This is true even if there are no crowds of people protesting new mansions in the suburbs, because it's the ordinary "right" place for money to be spent. America is a free-market, capitalist society. Regardless, keep in mind that most new residents, especially ex-suburbanites who move to the city, are vilified as the face of gentrification. Make sure your face is clean.

Most cities that want to survive know that they must increase their middle-class populations. Still, new city dwellers *must* realize a very important fact about their new lives and new neighborhood—it's not a subdivision. If you decide to move to the city, make sure to do it as responsibly and ethically as is possible. Integrate responsibly and enthusiastically blend into your new neighborhood. Your new neighbors may even ask you over for dinner!

The Responsible Urban Integration Pledge

I pledge that in my move to the city I will:

Choose to live in a structure that displaces no one. *If you're buying a build-ing that houses families who will be forced to move, ask questions, possibly even rethink your decision. Ask about the family or individuals who live in a house or building that's for sale—and whether they are being forced out by this sale. Abandoned homes and buildings with no residents may be available. New build-ings on vacant properties or old parking lots are safe bets. The goal is not to knowingly kick anyone out for the sake of one financial transaction—especially if there are good alternatives.*

Meet as many of my neighbors as possible. *Sit down with them and tell why you have chosen city life. Ask about their history in the neighborhood as well. Exchange phone numbers. Ask them over. Have a dinner party or a cook-out for your new neighborhood. Get involved and in tune with the people you chose to live around.*

Volunteer in my new community. *Join a neighborhood watch. Attend a local church. Become a regular at community meetings. In as many ways as possible, actually become a community member instead of an uninvolved squatter. Con-sider establishing volunteer agencies to meet one or more community needs.*

Find my own ways to make my chosen neighborhood better than it was before I came. *Use your creativity to make the neighborhood real, inclusive, and special. Make sure you can list many examples of positive contributions that you have made personally. Don't wall yourself in.*

Embrace and welcome many kinds of people as neighbors after I become "local" myself. *Creating labels and stereotypes for people groups is a part of human nature. Try to use your new city living experience to see people as neigh-bors, not as stereotypes.*

Understand that I, alone, cannot change the world. *But consciously do your part to make your little piece of the world a gentler, more authentic place.*

Enjoy my urban life. *Revel in your new city atmosphere, which is so different from the life you left behind in the suburbs.*

Signature:

_____

FIND URBAN KIDS FOR YOUR URBAN KIDS

One of the best reasons many city lovers have for staying in the suburbs is that they have or plan to have children. Cites have long been considered less than an ideal setting to raise kids, and it is true that, historically, most families with children overwhelmingly choose the suburbs. Cities don't have big backyards, woods, and endless open spaces for kids to frolic. Apartments and houses are usually much smaller in the city as well. Because of all of these things, suburbs have become incubators for Americans.

Probably the number one reason for parents to choose suburban homes is the schools. Indeed, inner-city public school systems are often less than desirable, scoring much lower in educational quality and test scores than their suburban counterparts. Even with this hindrance, some families are finding ways to raise their children successfully in an urban environment. Families that can afford private schools find that the most prestigious ones are located in the city. Public magnet schools where highly creative learning experiences are offered are often in the downtown and surrounding neighborhoods. Some homeschool. Others enroll their children in the ailing public schools, but commit themselves to highly involved volunteerism. These families consider their action to be a part of the solution, actively contributing to the health of city schools (and the city itself), instead of retreating to the suburbs.

Some parents realize that their city kids have many advantages. If children aren't old enough to drive, they still have the freedom to move—via buses, bikes, trains, walking, etc.—to all kinds of destinations. Walking to school the old-fashioned way is also possible. Because of this freedom, city kids are often more independent, responsible, and aware of their surroundings.

Still, it can be daunting to have children in the city. Suburban parents may fear that their children's freedom might get them into trouble or put them in danger. They're not alone.

Many urbs with large influxes of families with children establish formal "kid networks" and hold scheduled meetings, events, and playtime in the park. Urban families have the advantage of the strong camaraderie that comes with the decision to move to the city and often form strong and lasting bonds with other similar families.

Counting kids after a face painting and balloon sculpting session in River Market, Kansas City.

The key to successful integration of children into an urban neighborhood is smart family positioning. Before you decide on a neighborhood, one of the first things you should do is to take a walk with your kids. Keep an eye out for other families with children. Note the child-friendliest spots. Map out a central location near a park, school, neighborhood store, library, children's theater, and other kid attractions. Think about where and how your children will use these services.

A great way to decide on a kid-friendly neighborhood is to introduce yourself and your children to others on a playground or sidewalk, swap phone numbers, ask about other families and their situation, and judge the overall environment. Doing this kind of research can uncover a great place to raise kids. Despite the long-standing school quality problem, blindly accepting that suburbia is always best for kids may cause your family to miss an opportunity. Investigating an urban neighborhood is the only way to find out.

PREPARE FOR A LIFE ADVENTURE

Moving to the authentic city from the suburbs is for "weirdos." This is because everyone seems to be planning their next move farther out, perhaps to the country, while the weirdos are packing moving vans and heading in the opposite direction. Instead of life in new subdivisions and the popular backyard view of as-yet-undeveloped land, weirdos are seeking inspirational, authentic urban places full of life and new experiences.

You've made the decision to become a weirdo. Expect to meet and become friends with all kinds of other weirdos. Anticipate exploring and learning from different cultures, ideologies, and ethnicities. Dream of walking electric urban corridors because that dream will come true soon. Expect the goose bumps that only urban energy can produce on a city lover's skin.

Visualize the skyline from a loft window. Plan on spending whole afternoons people watching at outdoor street cafés, meeting friends on the corner before a stroll to the grocery store, and dog walking with urban neighbors. Consider your new city life to be as exciting as a jungle safari, skiing, or skydiving. Get ready never to be bored again.

Prepare for an environment full of oomph that mirrors residents' energetic personalities. Anticipate taking advantage of your proximity to rousing nightlife, spontaneous music, and impromptu street drama just outside your door. Become part of an electric urban energy and vigorous city rhythm.

There is no more dramatic life event than moving from a cloistered cul-de-sac to the middle of a vibrant city. Being able to walk to nearby outdoor markets, neighborhood diners, corner grocery stores, or pushcart vendors is priceless. Though unimaginable now, a short trip down a staircase or elevator is all that's required to access food, stimulation, and, most of all—fun!

Get ready to grease up your bicycle, purchase a bus pass, and find your walking shoes. Prepare for nights of the opera, a comedy show, and perhaps a jazz festival or just a movie. Whatever event you choose, anticipate being surrounded by and living in art. Expect to have fun, and expect to be challenged as you've never been before.

Life adventures rarely are the result of repeating familiar patterns. The road to the city is the one less traveled. Allow yourself to become absorbed by urban energy. Think of the positive contribution you can make to your new neighborhood.

It is your responsibility as a new urb resident to contribute to the local energy in your own way. The city insists on it. Become active, vital, eventful, moody, and expressive. Volunteer scarce time and valuable talents. Accentuate your personality. Help reinvigorate the entire city. You'll become a dynamic part of a city neighborhood in of the most exciting and "real" urban revitalizations America has ever experienced. Congratulations! (Now go pack!)

CITIES ON YOUR LIST

Which cities and urbs (if currently known) are you planning on visiting in your search for home?

City: _____

Known urbs to visit:

_____

_____

_____

_____

City: _____

Known urbs to visit:

_____

_____

_____

_____

City: _____

Known urbs to visit:

_____

_____

_____

_____

City: _____

Known urbs to visit:

_____

_____

_____

_____

GLOSSARY

the authentic city: Dense places in and around the downtown having large areas of connected angular urban street shapes that support *urban behavior*.

Blank Canvas Urb: Area of the city that has latent urban energy. They are viewed in the same way that painters view their blank canvases—as being in a temporary state, simply needing a splash of color, creativity, and inspiration.

creative places: Funky places that encourage ideas to bounce off mortar and bricks and from mind to mind.

Detroit: The model city that resembles *Blank Canvas Urbs* across America.

Eclectic Urb: City neighborhood that has diverse architectural styles, quaint quiet enclaves, and roaring districts full of high energy. Most of all, *Eclectic Urbs* can be described as *funky places*.

fake urbs: Places that support urban behavior but are usually shopping malls that are not connected by the greater city. Fake urbs are actually urban *pods* that resemble authentic cities.

funky places: "Funky" is a combination of design features, people, activities, art, colors, behavior, functions, lifestyles, and other components that exist in a place that is skewed, often far left of normal. Among other elements, funky places have diverse populations, highly expressive personalities, overflowing art, varied architecture, and interesting special events.

Garden Urb: City neighborhood that has an abundance of urban parks, mature tree-lined streets, and a small-town feeling.

gentrification: Used mostly in a negative connotation meaning the middle class moving into a poor neighborhood and changing its character.

getting urban: Moving from a suburb or a subdivision into the authentic city and transforming your life.

Greenwich Village: America's original funky, *Eclectic Urb* in Lower Manhattan.

infill: Buildings constructed in existing neighborhoods, usually on vacant and surface parking lots, "filling in the blank spots."

in-town: A location specifying downtown and the neighborhoods surrounding it.

latent urban energy: Urban energy that is trapped inside empty city blocks and is usually associated with *Blank Canvas Urbs*.

life adventure: The process of transforming your life and *getting urban*.

loft: Lofts are apartments usually associated with *Postindustrial Urbs*. They have elevated bedrooms, concrete floors, high multipaned windows, exposed bricks and mortar, uncovered plumbing, and suspended air ducts. Loft interiors have open and airy designs with clean lines, sharp edges, steel beams, and ornamental rivets.

mallternative: Special corridors lined with businesses that feature interesting and sometimes alternative retail stores; these are often considered to be primary locations that define the rest of the neighborhood.

pods: Subdivisions and shopping centers in the suburbs that confine a specific activity to one location (like shops, houses, offices, parks, and others) and are usually connected to each other by only one point. Pods are designed intentionally to produce *suburban behavior*.

positioning yourself: The act of thinking about everything possible that will make an urban experience more functional, enjoyable, and urban, and then pinpointing the perfect location to move to. This location will ensure quality urban living around an individual's hobbies, shopping places, work, entertainment, and transportation.

Postindustrial Urb: City neighborhood resembling SoHo that has an edgy, minimalist, hard-knock ambience and is defined by loft apartments, steel and concrete, and outdoor markets.

responsible urban integration: Newcomers to the city who become contributing members of a reemerging neighborhood. A positive phenomenon and the opposite of the negative, pessimistic, toxic word and phenomenon, gentrification.

Savannah, Georgia: A lush, garden city that has become the model for *Garden Urbs* across America.

schlepping: A term many New Yorkers use to describe carrying things and a science that urbanites must master.

SoHo: The Lower Manhattan neighborhood full of lofts and old industrial buildings that has come to be a model for all *Postindustrial Urbs*.

suburban behavior: The act of moving from one *pod* to another, usually by driving everywhere, parking in huge surface lots, shopping at suburban commercial strips, obsessing about privacy, including private drives, privacy fences, and private space inside of cars.

suburban energy: Muted and reclusive human activity, vitality, events, moods, and expressions that are designed as such by separated buildings, wide streets, and hidden people.

suburban flaws: Personal and specific reasons why people want to move out of the suburbs.

suburban sprawl: Any pattern of development that discourages intense pedestrian activity; makes using buses, trains, cabs, and bicycles for functional purposes very difficult; deters one-on-one human interaction; and hinders sidewalk eating and conversing as well as any other behavior that would resemble city bustle.

suburban street shapes: Street shapes that look like cartoon characters or something other than a primary shape (such as squares, rectangles, triangles).

trendy: A term used mostly by suburbanites to explain the city's customs, architecture, transportation modes, and infrastructure, regardless of the fact that they are actually old-fashioned.

urb: An area of the city that is able to harness and distribute *urban energy*. Urbs are always places located on a street grid where people live, work, play, shop, and thrive (or places with the potential to do all of these activities).

urb brand: Logos and other images used to further interpret an *Urb*'s theme. Urb brands are used for image recognition, marketing, and luring new people and businesses to urban neighborhoods.

urb theme: A catchphrase and/or descriptive literature that local boosters use to define their neighborhoods.

urb type: See *Postindustrial, Garden, Eclectic, Blank Canvas.*

urban activism: A movement to save city neighborhoods from further deterioration and to encourage redevelopment and vitality. Urban activism is similar to causes such as saving the rain forest or eradicating animal abuse.

urban behavior: Intense pedestrian activity, using buses, trains, cabs, and bicycles for functional purposes, one-on-one human interaction, sidewalk eating and conversing, and any behavior that contributes to the general city bustle.

urban draws: Attractive aspects of city life that draw people to live there.

urban energy: The power generated and distributed by a city's activity, vitality, events, moods, and expressions that are sustained by the relationships among buildings, streets, and people.

urban grid: An ordered, rigid network of rectangles, squares, and triangles (and sometimes circles) that creates a web of angular city blocks.

urban optimism: A phenomenon in city neighborhoods that have an undying hope for a better tomorrow, despite the fact that they have been ravaged by abandonment, economic disinvestment, wrecking balls, crime, drugs, poverty, poor schools, weeds, litter, rodents, dilapidated buildings, and deteriorating infrastructures.

urban plan: Similar to a city's DNA and containing streets (like strands) that form a blueprint, guiding how the city will grow and what form it will take. The plan also governs the shape of the streets and the patterns they will create in forming city blocks.

Urban Quality Checklist: A tool for people who decide to move to the city that contains universal elements found in every quality urban environment. It provides the background information and perspectives needed to analyze an urban living environment critically.

urban street shapes: Squares, rectangles, triangles, and, sometimes, circles.

urban-suburban cost-of-living trade-off: The higher price per square foot of living space city dwellers must usually pay for an urban lifestyle.

urban values: The opposite of suburban values, these include such things as walking, biking, or using public transportation instead of driving; living in high-density neighborhoods instead of spacious subdivisions with big laws; appreciating historic, gritty places instead of new and clean subdivisions; and cheering new infill development instead of protesting new subdivisions.

weirdo: A person who is bored and unhappy stuck in the suburbs (the places where most so-called normal Americans live).

INDEX

ABOUT THE AUTHOR

Kyle Ezell, A.I.C.P., is a certified city planner and fervent crusader for urban living. He is currently Project Coordinator for Urban Revitalization in Columbus, Ohio, working closely with the Mayor's office, local neighborhood commissions, non-profit corporations, and developers to revitalize the city's inner neighborhoods. He was city planner for downtown Chattanooga involved in the planning, design, and implementation of the nationally acclaimed Tennessee Riverpark and Coolidge Park projects; and a city planner in Maryville, Tennessee and Dublin, Ohio. Certified by the American Institute of Certified Planners, he has been a speaker at the American Planning Association's regional conferences, and been interviewed by numerous newspaper and television media as an expert on revitalizing cities. He has a BS in business administration from the University of Tennessee, Knoxville and an MS in cultural geography from South Dakota State University. A dedicated city-lover, he lives in the eclectic Short North neighborhood of Columbus, Ohio.

Kyle is the founder of Get Urban America, an organization devoted to revitalizing cities with new urban dwellers and ideas. Get Urban America provides knowledgeable speakers for downtown business and residential development programs and organizations and consulting services to in-town developers who want to excite their potential residential buyers about city living. Find out more about Get Urban America and Kyle Ezell on *www.geturban.com*